Golf Digest

PERFECT YOUR SWING

A FIREFLY BOOK

Published by Firefly Books Ltd. 2004

Design and text copyright © 2001, 2004 Carlton Books Limited
Material reprinted by permission from Golf Digest®. Copyright ©
2001, 2004 The Golf Digest Companies.

First printing

Publisher Cataloging-in-Publication Data (U.S.)

Rudy, Matthew.
   Golf digest perfect your swing : learn to hit the ball like the
game's greats / Matthew Rudy.
[192] p. : col. photos. ; cm.
Summary: Guide and instruction book on how to improve your
golf swing featuring sequenced photographs of some of golf's
greatest players.

ISBN 1-55297-986-5 (pbk.)
   1. Swing (Golf).   2. Golf — Training. I. Title.
796.352/3 dc22   GV979.S9.R839   2004

National Library of Canada Cataloguing in Publication

Rudy, Matthew
   Golf digest, perfect your swing : learn to hit the ball like the
game's greats / Matthew Rudy.

ISBN 1-55297-986-5
   1. Swing (Golf) I. Title. II. Title: Perfect your swing.
GV979.S9R83 2004   796.352'3   C2004-901215-0

Published in the United States in 2004 by
Firefly Books (U.S.) Inc.
P.O. Box 1338, Ellicott Station
Buffalo, New York 14205

Published in Canada in 2004 by
Firefly Books Ltd.
66 Leek Crescent
Richmond Hill, Ontario L4B 1H1

Front Cover Photographs: Ernie Els and Sergio Garcia (©Golf
Digest 2001)

Back Cover Photographs: Greg Norman (all photographs and
licensed marks ©Golf Digest 2001)

First published under the title *Golf Digest: The Swing* in 2001

GOLF DIGEST is a registered trademark of Advance Magazine
Publishers Inc.

Printed in Singapore

Golf Digest

PERFECT YOUR
SWING

*Learn how to hit the ball
like the game's greats*

MATTHEW RUDY

FIREFLY BOOKS

Contents

The History of the Swing

When Bobby Jones said, "He plays a game with which I am not familiar," he was talking about Jack Nicklaus winning the 1965 Masters by nine shots. But Jones, who played his own incomparable game in 1929, could have been a player of any generation, looking on with appreciation at how things have changed over the years.

THE TOOLS USED TO PLAY GOLF EVEN AS RECENTLY AS 1850 are barely recognizable when compared to those used today. They were thick-shafted, one-piece poles with extended heads—more like hockey sticks than Great Big Berthas. The balls were barely-round leather pouches stuffed with feathers. The men using them wore woolen jackets that kept them from moving their arms much above waist level. A player who could hit one of these featheries 150 yards was considered a man of great strength. It should come as no surprise, then, that the first regular swing "style" in the game's history was a low, slow-moving, "handsy" swipe from a crouched stance that kept the ball low (below the Scottish winds) and rolling along the ground. Willie Park won the first British Open in 1860 using this combination of equipment, shooting a three-round score of 174 on a 12-hole course with a par of 48.

It wasn't until Allan Robertson devised a different way to build a club—with a slender wooden shaft and an iron head—that players could control the ball with anything more than a rudimentary degree of accuracy. It is a story that has repeated itself many times through the years. A smaller, weaker player needed some other way to compete with bigger, stronger golfers. Robertson built clubs that were lighter and more flexible—ones he could buggy-whip through impact. The combination of new materials and physics

Allan Robertson devised a new club with an iron head and flexible shaft.

could see consistent ball flight from a certain kind of strike, they started to experiment with ways to change that flight, curving shots to the right and left and imparting backspin to make the ball roll less after landing. One golfer who tried to make the most of the available technology was Tom Kidd, who won the 1873 British Open at St Andrews using irons he had built himself. They had spines of metal running across their faces, which created much more backspin than the common, smooth-faced irons that were being used at the time. They were quickly banned by the game's first ruling body, the Royal & Ancient—and even today, clubs must have nothing protruding from the face to conform with the rules.

Now that the game had developed the tools to perfect a swing that could dictate shots, it was time for a player to come along with enough talent to do the same. That player was Harry Vardon.

Vardon grew up caddieing for players who used the old-school technique, and he tried all kinds of varieties of that swing in his own game. But, like Robertson, he found that the lighter, shorter clubs gave him much better results, and he started experimenting with those. The shorter clubs forced him to make a much more upright swing. The photographs that remain of that swing show that it was indeed

helped him to hit his shots not only longer than his bigger competitors, but also with more accuracy. It provided the impetus for a new kind of swing—the prehistoric ancestor of Harry Vardon's upright, "modern" golf swing. Ball technology still had to catch up, though, and soon enough it did.

By the mid-1850s, balls made of gutta percha (a natural, balata-like substance) had all but replaced featheries. The gutties were manufactured by machine, which made them nice and round—and also far more consistent. When golfers

Harry Vardon popularized the "modern" upright swing and a grip that linked the hands together.

the precursor to the "modern" swing. Vardon was much more concerned with a rhythmic transition from backswing to downswing than anyone else in his day. Even with the limitations of his dress (those wool jackets were still *de rigeur*), Vardon made a full backswing, getting the club back over his right shoulder and turning his hips aggressively. His finish—aside from the bent right elbow—looks like one you might see today. Vardon was also the first player to popular-

ize a grip that linked the hands together. Before, when the wooden clubs were heavier and stiffer, a grip that had all ten fingers on the handle was critical to keeping the swing under control. But Vardon, using these lighter, whippier clubs, over-lapped the little finger on his right hand on the groove between the index and middle fingers on his left hand. That grip, the Vardon grip, is still the preferred way for 95 percent of the world's touring professionals to hold the club today.

As innovative as Vardon's ideas about the swing were, they wouldn't have had nearly the same impact if he hadn't had such an impressive record as a player. He won six British Opens between 1896 and 1914, and, as a result, was the premier ball and club endorser of his day—sort of like a Tiger Woods in a wool coat and knickers. One of those deals (with his sponsors, A.G. Spalding) was directly responsible for the infusion of Vardon's ideas on the other side of the Atlantic, in what would become the biggest golf market in the world. In 1900, Vardon made promotional trips to the United States to play in exhibitions (he covered almost 20,000 miles during the year) and to compete in the fledging US Open (which he won by two strokes). Vardon cut an exotic, dashing figure, setting course records wherever he went and inspiring average Americans to pick up the game. And when they did, of course, they copied both Vardon's grip and swing. One of those who watched and learned from Vardon was a kid trying to decide between a career as a golfer or a professional baseball player. Walter Hagen chose golf.

Thanks to Vardon, golf's popularity increased steadily in the United States througout the first two decades of the century. Americans were thirsting for instruction—and had the money to pay for it. This caused an exodus of talented (and some not-so-talented) Englishmen, Scots and Irishmen to the practice ranges and resorts across the Atlantic. One of them, Jim Barnes, won the first two PGA Championships played, in 1916 and 1919, and the 1921 US Open. He capitalized on those successes by producing one of the game's first golf instruction books, featuring slow-motion photography of Barnes' swing, detailed photographs of the equipment he used and advice about playing the game. Another of those emigrating Scots was Donald Ross, who relocated to North Carolina and built dozens of courses—including Pinehurst No. 2—that still rank among the greatest in America. A third was Stewart Maiden, who came to East Lake Golf Club in Atlanta and taught a young man called Bobby Jones.

Ben Hogan dug his swing from the dirt.

In the 1920s, a professional golf tour had yet to be established. Stars like Walter Hagen and Gene Sarazen played exhibitions around the country, competed in national events like the US Open and PGA Championship, and, in Sarazen's case, taught lessons at a home club in the off-season. As a result, an entire generation of instructors received their education in the game directly from the most accomplished players of the era. Henry Picard, a great player in the 1920s, 30s and 40s, taught Jack Grout, who would in turn go on to develop Jack Nicklaus' game. The great players of the 1940s and 1950s—Ben Hogan, Byron Nelson and Jimmy Demaret—all got into the game as assistant teaching professionals.

Professionals in the 1940s were also the first to play with steel-shafted clubs—the first quantum leap in equipment design since the guttie had been replaced by balata-covered balls filled with windings in 1905. Before steel, clubs had been made with hickory shafts—the same material used to make baseball bats. But hickory was expensive and it warped when it got wet. Added to that, it took an incredible level of craftsmanship to fit the shafts into a set of clubs. On the other hand, steel was cheap, it didn't warp, shafts made from it could be mass produced and it didn't whip and torque like hickory. Good players quickly realized that they could keep their wrists cocked longer in the downswing, swing harder and get longer and more consistent shots.

Byron Nelson was one of the first professionals to embrace steel. The upright swing that Nelson used to win 11 tournaments in a row in 1945—one that could rely on centrifugal force and the exponential power of the cocking and uncocking of the wrists—looked a lot like the swing tour players use today. Johnny Miller won eight tournaments in 1974 with Spalding irons that were virtually identical to the ones that Nelson used in 1945.

By the 1950s, professional golf had grown to the point that it could support a flourishing tour. All of a sudden, players like Ben Hogan—who had had to augment his tournament earnings with a club job—could play the tour almost full time. After ten years of struggle with a hook—and two years in the service during World War II—Hogan finally dug the secret out of the dirt. He rolled the clubface open on the backswing, then started to square it in the downswing as he hit against a firm left side. Hitting it left was never a problem again, and Hogan became the dominant player of his era. He also wrote an instruction book, *The Modern Fundamentals of Golf*, that would change the average recreation player's approach to learning the game. Hogan was convinced that any player who was in reasonably good

Following page:
The results for Hogan
were impressive.

shape and had moderate athletic ability could shoot near par if he followed Hogan's precise plan. Hogan didn't change the way golfers swung the club as much as he transformed the game—and the swing—into something that could be conquered through exhaustive analysis. If you worked hard enough, you could play well. Practicing could cure any problem, and preparation and study were the answer to shooting a good score. A horrific car accident and problems with his putting kept Hogan from winning to the degree he might have, but it didn't take long for players to embrace Hogan's principles and take them to that next level. Average players could now afford to buy high-quality, steel-shafted clubs at a reasonable price, and they had the modern swings of their heroes to copy and books from which to get the advice.

Hogan's swing was by far the most well-known through the 1950s, but it might not have been the most technically proficient. Mickey Wright didn't get much exposure on the LPGA Tour, but she should have. Wright won 82 tournaments between 1955 and 1973 (including four US Opens) and had what many consider to be the best swing of all time, man or woman. Her swing actually foreshadowed the kind of action that would become the standard for men and women start-

ing in the 1980s—an efficient, upright swing with no extra moving parts. It wouldn't look out of place on either tour today. Wright's accomplishments are all the more extraordinary considering that equipment companies didn't do much to build specialized clubs for female players. Wright did what she did with an ordinary set of men's, stiff-shafted irons, and because she was powerful enough not to have to make any adjustments to try and generate more distance, her swing is a perfect model for good players of either sex. Most modern PGA Tour players would win more money if they could strike the ball as well as Wright did 50 years ago.

The only thing missing for the average player was a way to see great swings in action—whether they belonged to Hogan or Wright. Sure, he could watch the pro at his local club play, or, if he was lucky enough to live in the right place, go and see a professional event in his hometown, but with the growth of television—and sports on television—golfers would soon be able to see all of their favorite players swing the club in vivid black-and-white from the comfort of their living room. And one man more than any other was responsible for getting golf on television on a weekly basis—Arnold Palmer. That Palmer had such an ungainly swing was

Previous page:
Bobby Jones' success in the 1920s turned golf into a spectator sport.

Arnold Palmer's photogenic style endeared him to millions.

Following page:
Jack Nicklaus dominated the game from 1961 to the early 1980s.

great for the game, even if it was bad for the way the average player played the game. That's because Palmer seemed to hit the ball with the same ungainly lunge that the average hack used. This, along with Palmer's everyman attitude and go-for-broke style, endeared him to millions of fans. They may not have picked the best swing to copy, but it certainly kept teaching pros in business. And when Palmer started having regular battles with the game's newest, biggest hitter, Jack Nicklaus, the drama could only be good for the growing sport.

Two things conspired to make Jack Nicklaus the game's greatest player: he had the drive to succeed; and he had a teacher who gave him a revolutionary way of accomplishing those lofty goals. Nicklaus was a big, stocky kid with plenty of power. From the beginning, Nicklaus' teacher, Jack Grout, encouraged him to swing as hard as he could. Grout's mantra was that distance was something you needed to

develop early, whereas accuracy could be taught later. Nicklaus, though, was the first student he had who could take the lesson and apply it so directly. By the time Nicklaus was in college at Ohio State, he was causing the same kind of stir with his game as Tiger Woods would 40 years later. Nicklaus was prodigiously long off the tee, thanks to some modifications in the "modern" swing he put into place with the help of Grout. Instead of cocking his wrists early in the backswing and "setting" them (like Hogan or Nelson), Nicklaus extended his arms as much as he could on the way back, extending the arc of his swing. He cocked his wrists much later, and he let his right elbow stick up, away from his chest, when he got to the top. This helped him to get his hands further away from his body than any other player and to fully coil his upper body. The huge arc gave him plenty of time to generate incredible clubhead speed. Nicklaus also used his thick legs to drive through the ball at impact and he finished with his hands high as he hit balls out of sight. He won everything there was to win as an amateur and almost won the 1960 US Open when he was a junior at Ohio State. Nicklaus played the final round with Hogan, who said afterward that Nicklaus would have won the tournament "if he had a brain in his head." Of course, Nicklaus did get it together upstairs—he was the game's ultimate course manager and chess master—and, once he did, he ran off a stretch of 20 seasons that has yet to be approached. From 1961 to 1986, Nicklaus won 18 professional majors, had 17 consecutive seasons with a win and earned eight money titles. He also became the most influential player in the game. Nicklaus' instruction book, *Golf My Way*, has sold more copies than any other golf instruction book in history. Hundreds of thousands of recreational players have adjusted their grip to be in a stronger position and tried to get a little bit more arc on their swings because of Nicklaus' words. And Nicklaus' deliberate style—he stepped off yardage on every shot—might have done more to cause slow play than any other single factor. Millions of hackers started pacing off distances, too, just like their hero.

It wasn't just a generation of average players that was inspired to try to copy Nicklaus. As in any era, the professionals who wanted to beat the best adopted some of the characteristics of the best player. Nicklaus hit the ball high and long—perfect for landing shots hit with longer clubs on fast greens. Throughout the 1970s, the best players (with the

Tom Watson was Nicklaus' main foil in the late 1970s and early 1980s.

Following page: Tiger Woods' swing is a snapshot of golf's future.

exception of Lee Trevino and Raymond Floyd, who were both self-taught) played with a swing that featured the head well back at impact (mostly because of active leg drive) and the hands high through the finish. Tom Watson, Johnny Miller and Tom Weiskopf all finished in the "reverse C" position. Even Greg Norman swung this way in his early days as a professional. But the major problem with the "reverse C" finish was that it was hard on the back. Nicklaus has never moved away from it, and he's had back problems throughout his senior career. Weiskopf and Watson tweaked their swings so that they hit against a firm left leg and finished in a more upright, back-friendly position.

If anyone is the model for the way the best players swing now (and will swing in the near future), it is Tiger Woods. Woods is the first of a new wave of tall, athletic players who can create incredible clubhead speed and take advantage of new developments in club technology to hit the ball longer than it has ever been hit before. Woods incorporates all of the things that made Nicklaus so long—great extension away from the ball, a full coil in the backswing—with lean, fast-firing muscles and longer, lighter, more forgiving clubs to make all but the longest par-fives obsolete. Nicklaus was hitting middle-irons into the par-fives at Augusta National in the mid-1960s—when the lofts on irons were weaker than they are today—but Woods is hittting into those same holes with 9-irons and wedges. Johnny Miller estimates that between his driver and 3 wood, he can hit it 30 yards longer now as a Senior Tour player on par-fives, than he could during his prime. The best players in the women's game—Annika Sorenstam, Se Ri Pak and Karrie Webb—get the same kind of extension and coil in their swings as Woods. Grace Park generates more power pound-for-pound than Woods, carrying drives 275 yards, even with a 5-foot-6, 125-pound frame. The future doesn't look good for the short hitter.

The Players

PROFESSIONAL ATHLETES WILL ALWAYS TALK ABOUT THE PRESSURE *of following up a championship win or another great performance. The level of expectation is always so much higher. Paul Azinger never had the luxury of being able to worry about those kinds of things. He had just reached the pinnacle of any golfer's career—winning a major championship, the 1993 PGA at Inverness—before he was diagnosed with cancer at the end of the same year.*

Paul Azinger

He lost his hair and a lot of weight, but was able to beat the lymphoma in his right shoulder blade and missed only most of the 1994 season. But when he won for the first time after the cancer, at the 2000 Sony Open, the satisfaction he felt was tempered by grief. His best friend on tour, Payne Stewart, had been killed in a plane crash three months earlier. "It's difficult to feel the same amount of joy I used to feel, like when I won the PGA Championship—that unencumbered joy," Azinger said. "I was seeing life through rose-colored glasses. I'm not wearing those anymore, but I'm still pretty happy."

Actually, when Azinger came back from illness, it wasn't the first time he had beaten the odds. As a high school player in Florida, he couldn't break 40 until he was a senior and wasn't recruited. After playing junior college golf and working with John Redman, Azinger's game blossomed and he transferred to Florida State, where he was an All-American in 1981. He lost his card in his first try at the PGA Tour in 1982, and spent the 1983 season playing minitours. He lost his card again in 1984, but won the PGA Tour Qualifying tournament that winter and has been a fixture ever since. He won three times in 1987, and at least once every year until 1993, when he exploded to second on the money list. He beat Corey Pavin by a single shot to win the prestigious Memorial Tournament and also took the New England Classic. His victory at the PGA was an instant classic. He caught both Greg Norman and Nick Faldo in regulation (by shooting a final-round 68), then beat Norman on the second hole of the play-off when Norman's four-footer for par lipped out. Based on how he had played the six years before, it isn't a stretch to think that Azinger would have won more than one major championship had he not been diagnosed with cancer. Regardless, he's just happy to be back.

1

2

3

4

5

6

7

8

*"Twelve years ago, I'd never broken 70 and
I couldn't break 80 two days in a row."*

Paul Azinger, *the night he won the 1993 PGA Championship.*

COMPARE PAUL AZINGER'S SWING TO THAT OF A STANDARD

PGA Tour player and almost nothing is similar. Even his set-up looks more like a ten-handicapper's than one that has won somebody more than $10 million. His grip is by far the strongest on tour. Two knuckles showing on the left hand is a standard, strong grip and Azinger has four showing. He felt so self-conscious about his grip when he first joined the tour that he seriously considered switching it. Redman, his teacher, convinced him to leave it alone, and he did, with great results. Azinger also plays the ball near the middle of his stance, even here with a driver. Most players set up with the ball just off the left toe. Because of that strong grip, the rest of Azinger's swing is designed to keep him from hooking it off the world. He's trying to keep the clubhead from turning over. "Through impact he holds on for dear life to keep from hitting a duck hook," says Johnny Miller. You can see how he slides his hips through impact in pictures 5 and 6, another anti-hook move.

1

2

3

4

5

6

7

8

YOU CAN SEE IN HIS SET UP THAT AZINGER INTENTIONALLY
aims to the left of the target. With all of his anti-hook moves, he tries to
play a low power fade. At impact, Azinger's right arm is significantly under
his left. If he didn't have it there, the club would come through closed and
send the ball dead left.

After impact, Azinger's body is a "reverse C" position that was more
common in the 1970s than it is now. That doesn't stop him from making a
full, balanced followthrough. In fact, he turns his shoulders completely
around and almost parallel to the target line, which shows both how full
his body release is and how flexible he is.

By the time Azinger finished his three-win 1993
season, he had risen to second on the
PGA Tour's all-time earnings list.
At that point, he was considered the best
American player in the world.

1

2

3

4

AS ODD AS AZINGER'S GRIP IS, YOU CAN SEE HERE HOW IT
helps him make a repeatable swing. His right shoulder is forced much lower than his left and inside the target line because of his grip. When he makes his backswing, all he has to do is turn his upper body and lift his arms. You can see in frames 2 and 4 that his swing plane changes from somewhat flat to more upright. But when you compare frame 2 to frame 5, he's on exactly the same plane halfway into his backswing as he is halfway down to impact. The most unique position Azinger gets in is the one he's in at impact. Most players have overlapping forearms at impact, but with Azinger, you can see a big gap between his arms. That's because his grip is so strong.

"Paul proves that most players would be better off working on the swing that their instincts tell them to use rather than trying to learn a one-dimensional swing that really isn't them."

Johnny Miller

5

6

7

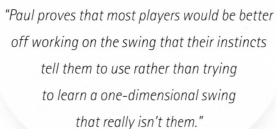

8

SEVE BALLESTEROS HAS SOME OF THE MOST MAGICAL HANDS *in the history of the game. He has astonished practice-round playing partners by smoothly lofting a shot out of a greenside bunker with a 3-iron and stopping it by the hole, and has won a British Open by driving wildly into a parking lot, slashing the recovery shot onto the green and still making birdie. "Seve can shoot a 64 a hundred different ways," said Nick Price.*

Seve Ballesteros

But more important than any of the five majors he has won (the 1979, 1984 and 1988 British Opens and 1980 and 1983 Masters), or any of the 67 other tournaments victories worldwide, Ballesteros single-handedly made the European Tour a viable enterprise and rescued the Ryder Cup from complete irrelevance. He won his first British Open as a cocky 22 year-old, then dominated golf in Europe for the next ten years, forcing sponsors both to increase purses and to pay appearance fees to attract the charismatic and popular Spaniard. For the people who play and follow the game in Europe, Ballesteros is as important a figure as Arnold Palmer is in the United States.

By 1979, the United States was regularly thumping its Great Britain and Ireland counterpart in the Ryder Cup, causing widespread disinterest among both fans and the media. That same year, Ballesteros was the hottest young player in the game. To add some more competition—and excitement—to the event, the Great Britain and Ireland team decided to expand and include players from the rest of the European continent. Of course, Ballesteros was conveniently eligible to play in the 1981 matches. The Europeans, led by Ballesteros and his young Spanish counterpart, Jose Maria Olazabal, then won back-to-back cups in 1985 and 1987. Each event since then has been a hard-fought struggle. It was only fitting that in 1997, when the matches were played for the first time outside the US or Great Britain, it was in Spain, at Valderrama, with Ballesteros as the European captain leading his side to victory. Ballesteros' increasing influence in the hierarchy of European golf has helped to alleviate at least a little bit of the frustration he has felt about his own game since 1995, when he won his last European event.

1 2 3 4

Ballesteros has won 78 tournaments worldwide— including the Opens of nine different countries: The Netherlands, France, Switzerland, Great Britain, Spain, Ireland, Germany, Japan and Kenya.

UNTIL HE REALLY STARTED TO STRUGGLE IN THE MID-1990s, BALLESTEROS had never given a thought to swing mechanics. His swing wasn't too different from the one he had learned as a child, crafting shots with a 3-iron on the beach near his home in Pedrena, Spain. It was a swing that relied completely on feel and timing. "Striking the ball cleanly from the sand teaches you great touch and clubhead control," Ballesteros said. "You have to hit the ball first, then the sand. And to do that, you have to stay steady through the swing." Ballesteros' swing is very upright—halfway into the backswing he has the club nearly perpendicular to the ground—which keeps him from releasing the club naturally. Instead, he uses a lot of hand action through impact—as you can see between pictures 6 and 7. That requires exceptional timing. If he's off a little bit, Ballesteros is wild off the tee both left and right—something that's happened with even more frequency over the last five years.

5 6 7 8

NOBODY HAS EVER QUESTIONED FRED COUPLES' TALENT.

His natural, unconventional swing produces huge drives and high, precise iron shots and he has stretches where he seems to sink every putt he looks at. But Couples has battled both back injuries and ambivalence about committing to the practice and travel required to win multiple major championships. As a result, his record is a patchwork of brilliant flashes and disappointing stretches.

Fred Couples

Regardless of the unevenness of Couples' play over his 20-year career, he remains one of the PGA Tour's most popular players because of his laid-back attitude and unassuming manner. Couples grew up in Seattle playing at Jefferson Park, a nine-hole municipal course. He never had any serious instruction, so he developed his trademark loose-limbed swing on his own to get enough distance to keep up with the older kids. Couples was an all-around athlete in high school and thought about playing professional baseball, but he took a golf scholarship at the University of Houston. The highlight of his time there might have been rooming with PGA Tour player Blaine McCallister and CBS commentator Jim Nantz. Couples made it onto the PGA Tour in 1981 and was a solid, mid-level player for the next ten years. He first showed his potential by winning the 1983 Kemper Open and the 1984 Players Champion-

ship, where he beat Lee Trevino by a shot. Couples didn't fully emerge as a superstar until eight years later, in 1992, when he went on a six-tournament run that would secure his place as a fan-favorite. Starting with the LA Open, Couples won three tournaments and finished second in two others over the six events. The centerpiece of the run was the Masters. There, he shot a final-round 70 to win by two shots over Raymond Floyd. That stretch was enough to carry him to the money title and a PGA Tour Player of the Year award. After several years of indifferent results, Couples rededicated himself to tournament golf in 2003. With some help from Butch Harmon, Couples sharpened his swing and had his best results in a long time. He won the Shell Houston Open and finished 34th on the money list, reviving hope that he can win one more major.

1

2

3

4

ACCORDING TO JOHNNY MILLER, PROFESSIONAL GOLFERS FALL

into two categories: some, like himself, have to understand what's happening in the swing; others, like Fred Couples, play what Miller calls "caveman golf. See ball. Hit ball." Part of what has made Couples so successful is that he doesn't complicate things for himself. He disdains swing thoughts and swing keys. Instead, he keeps his mind clear and lets things flow. That kind of approach works particularly well with Couples' self-taught, feel-oriented swing. It also helps to be mind-bogglingly flexible. John Daly might be the only other person in golf who could get into Couples' position in frame 4. He's got his back to the target while his hips have barely turned—and his left foot is flat on the ground. No wonder he's struggled with back problems. What also stands out is Couples' exceptionally strong grip—the top of his hand is on the top of the club. That allows him to keep the incredible wrist cock on the downswing. Combine that late release with the speed of his hip rotation between frames 4 and 5 and it's easy to see how Couples hits the ball so long.

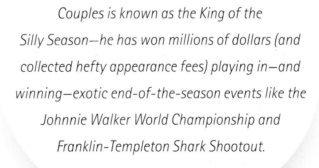

Couples is known as the King of the Silly Season—he has won millions of dollars (and collected hefty appearance fees) playing in—and winning—exotic end-of-the-season events like the Johnnie Walker World Championship and Franklin-Templeton Shark Shootout.

5

6

7

8

1

2

3

4

FROM HERE, YOU CAN SEE HOW, IN FRAME 2, COUPLES TAKES THE club slightly to the outside to start his backswing. From this position, he can make a little loop at the top that will bring the club through the ball from inside to out. In frame 4, look how far he is able to get his right arm behind his body. It's another example of a position most golfers couldn't dream of getting into. From the top, he makes a slow transition to the downswing, because his hands need time to get out from behind his head. If he went too quick here, the club would have no place to go but over the top.

In 1995, Couples became the first PGA Tour player to win back-to-back events on the European Tour (the Johnnie Walker Classic and Dubai Desert Classic) since Charlie Coody in 1973.

5

6

7

8

1

2

3

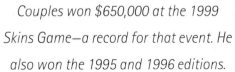

4

AS UNIQUE AS COUPLES' SWING IS, HE STILL DOES A LOT OF things right. His right elbow "flies" at the top of the backswing, but by the time he is halfway through the downswing, that right elbow is glued to his right hip—exactly where it should be—and the club perfectly bisects the triangle created by his two forearms. At impact, his left side is nicely braced, and he's kept his spine angle the same since address. See how the shaft and his right arm form a straight line at impact? He'll hit a high, controlled fade.

Couples won $650,000 at the 1999 Skins Game—a record for that event. He also won the 1995 and 1996 editions.

5

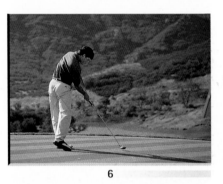

6

7

8

IN A WORLD WHERE PERFECT, CONTROLLED SWINGS ARE MADE *by often indistinguishable players, John Daly stands out, both literally and figuratively. We could leave the captions out on these four pages and you could identify the man in these pictures, even if we blurred the face. "Throw away the book," said* Golf Digest *teaching professional Rick Smith. "His athletic ability, flexibility, hands, it's phenomenal."*

John Daly

4

Like good folklore, Daly's story has been well-told. He drove all night just to get to the 1991 PGA Championship at Crooked Stick, when he made it into the field as the last-minute, ninth alternate. The first time he had ever seen—let alone played—the course was the first round of the tournament. Daly, a rookie, shot 69-67-69-71 to win by three strokes, hitting drives out of sight in the process. His everyman appeal wasn't any act. A native of Rogers, Arkansas, he really was everyman. He signed autographs until there was nobody left to sign for. Before Tiger Woods arrived, he was the PGA Tour's most popular player with fans.

As popular as he was, though, Daly was still considered the "fluke" major winner by players and the golf media. That perception changed in 1995, when he won golf's most venerated

championship at its most venerated site—the British Open at St Andrews. Almost as shocking as Daly winning was the way in which he won, with controlled aggression, precise shot-making and touch on and around the greens that Seve would have been proud of. Keeping with the folklore theme, even the ending was the stuff of legends. Costantino Rocca holed a 70-foot putt from off the green—after chili-dipping his chip—to force a playoff. But Daly came out on top after a four-hole playoff to become only the fourth American (Woods has since become the fifth) to win two majors before his 30th birthday.

Troubles with alcohol and weight derailed Daly in the late 1990s, but by 2001 he seemed to have regained control. Through it all, the swing hasn't changed. He still grips it and rips it.

1

2

3

4

Daly has won the driving distance title nine times, including six years in a row (1995-2000). In 2000, he was the only player to average more than 300 yards per drive (301.4).

THE AMAZING THING ABOUT DALY'S SWING IS THAT AS EXAGGERATED AS IT is, technically, it's very sound. His address position is straightforward. Power hitters have two things in common at address—a strong grip and the head significantly behind the ball. You can see from the tilt in his shoulders that he's preparing for a sweeping upward blow at the ball, which is critical for long, high drives. Frame 4 is the classic one. In addition to a huge turn, he also has incredibly flexible wrists, which let him cock the club so dramatically behind his back. Daly is the only player in the history of the game who has been able to make consistent contact from this unbelievable position—most people who try this end up in traction. At impact, you can see just how far his head is behind his body and how he has braced his left side to pivot against it. Daly has such good balance, he's never out of control, even with such a violent swing.

5

6

7

8

1

2

3

4

FROM ABOVE, IT'S VERY EASY TO SEE JUST HOW much turn Daly gets in his backswing. When he struggles, it's usually because of inconsistencies in his long swing. *Golf Digest* teaching professional David Leadbetter has said he believes Daly could shorten his swing without sacrificing much distance, if any at all. He could become more consistent and save the wear and tear on his back. Daly's swing is almost certainly one that won't age well, even if he stays as flexible as he can. Most Senior Tour players aren't getting the club back to parallel on the backswing, much less scratching their backs with the club like Daly does. In the second frame, you can see how far away Daly's hands are from his body. He's creating a huge arc, another power key.

"His terrific balance as everything winds down indicates how well-coordinated his actions are at all points of the swing, despite their great force." **Jack Nicklaus**, *on John Daly's swing.*

5

6

7

8

1   2   3   4

One of Daly's favorite pro-am tricks is to hit a tee shot with his putter—275 yards. If that doesn't sufficiently impress the paying customers, he then launches a 240-yard 6-iron out of sight.

UNLIKE MOST TOUR PLAYERS, DALY HAS RARELY sought help from a teacher for swing problems. His swing is self-taught—even as he was winning the 1991 PGA, he said the only swing thought he ever had was "kill." Since his swing is so reliant on feel, flexibility and natural athleticism, not to mention the fact that it's so different from anything else out there, Daly has tried to solve his problems by working them out himself on the range, or by experimenting with his equipment. Like most power hitters, Daly prefers to hit a high fade and the shot he tries to avoid at all costs is a hard hook. Daly sprays his tee shots when his aggressive arm swing, which you can see in frames 4 and 5, gets out of sync with his hip turn. At the finish, you can see how long it takes to dissipate all the power Daly has generated. If he didn't wear spikes, he might corkscrew himself into the ground.

5   6   7   8

NONE OF THE MONEY COUNTED TOWARD ANY OFFICIAL LIST,
but when Laura Davies and John Daly paired to win the mixed-team JCPenney Classic in 1999, it was the most appropriate victory of the season. The two are kindred spirits. Both are self-taught, free-wheeling, full-tilt bashers of the golf ball, both like to have a good time off the course and both are among the most popular players on their respective tours.

Laura Davies

Davies was beating balls into submission on the LPGA Tour—and before that on the Women's Professional Golf European Tour (WPGET)—long before Daly made it on to the PGA Tour. So before anyone calls Davies the women's tour's version of Daly, perhaps the comparison should be reversed.

Davies was a celebrated amateur in Great Britain, where she won the 1983 English Intermediate Championship and the 1983 and '84 South Eastern Championships. She turned pro at age 22, in 1985, and immediately led the WPGET in earnings as a rookie and again in her second season. In 1987, while still playing full-time in Europe, she won the US Women's Open in a play-off with Ayako Akamoto and Joanne Carner. But, by the Byzantine LPGA rules of the time, the win didn't make her exempt into any other LPGA events. Sensing that the charismatic, long-hitting Davies would add star

power to the tour, though, the LPGA amended its constitution and gave Davies membership. She has played full-time in America ever since.

The odd circumstances surrounding Davies' immigration to the US Tour were accentuated the next season, when the defending Women's Open champion won two more events and was named the LPGA rookie of the year. Throughout the 1990s, Davies was a major force in the women's game, winning three more major championships, the 1994 and 1996 McDonald's LPGA Championships and the 1996 duMaurier. Her win at the 2000 Los Angeles Women's Championship (her 60th tournament victory worldwide), only added to her legend. Davies underwent LASIK eye surgery four days before the tournament started, showed up in Los Angeles, and without the benefit of a practice round shot 67, 71 and 73 to win by three strokes. She gives the LPGA needed personality.

1

5

2

6

A devoted sports fan, Davies carries a small television in her bag when her favorite soccer team is playing a crucial match. She checks in on the action when there's a wait on the tee.

3

7

LIKE DALY, HER COUNTERPART ON THE MEN'S TOUR, DAVIES HAS

never spent much time thinking about the intricacies of her swing. "Tempo and strike. That's all I'm thinking about," she said. In fact, she rarely spends time on the practice range. "I never really play that badly," Davies said. "Striking the ball well has always been easy for me. The hard part is scoring." Davies sets up to the ball as an athlete. She plays the ball more toward the middle of her stance than many other professionals, but still has a nice straight line from her left shoulder down to the ball. She kicks her left knee back away from the target dramatically in frames 3 and 4 to help generate some extra shoulder turn. As a result, she gets the club back dramatically behind her, well past parallel. Davies' struggles come when she doesn't synchronize her swing from this point and accelerates too soon on the downswing.

4

8

1

2

3

4

PART OF HITTING THE BALL A LONG WAY IS HAVING THE
physical makeup to do it, and Davies does. She's got wide shoulders and strong thighs and quads. She's one of the few female players who simply overpower the ball. Other long hitters, like Grace Park, have to do it purely with technique. Davies' trademark is her position at impact. She actually hunches forward, toward the ball a little bit, but offsets this move by getting up on her toes. She looks like she's going to explode out of her shoes. Davies' swing is high-effort. You can really tell she's putting a whack on the ball.

In 1996, Davies won four times on the LPGA and was second on the money list, while simultaneously winning the WPGET's money title in Europe.

5

6

7

8

1

2

3

4

5

6

7

8

DAVIES DOESN'T WAIT LONG TO START COILING INTO HER BACK-
swing. In frame 2, she's already started to turn her shoulders—the difference in
her left shoulder position between frames 1 and 2 is distinct. In frame 3, Davies
looks a lot like Jack Nicklaus, with the flying right elbow, cocked left knee and
high hands. Her shoulder turn through impact is so violent that she loses
control over the lower half of her body. It gives her so many problems that she
rarely hits her driver any more. Of course, she doesn't really need to. She
averaged more than 250 yards off the tee in 2000 using mostly 2- and 3-irons.

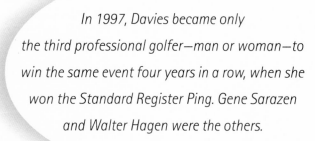

*In 1997, Davies became only
the third professional golfer—man or woman—to
win the same event four years in a row, when she
won the Standard Register Ping. Gene Sarazen
and Walter Hagen were the others.*

FEW PLAYERS HAVE TRANSFORMED THEMSELVES AS COMPLETELY

as David Duval in such a short period of time. From the time his wildly successful 1999 season was over to the 2000 Mercedes Championships two months later, Duval remade his body. He went from a stocky 220 pounds to a lean, sculptured 180, and even signed a deal with a cutting edge surf-wear company to show off his new physique in collarless golf shirts and tight pants.

David Duval

And Duval did all of this when his game was at his peak—11 wins in a little over two years, including a surreal stretch where he won four times before the 1999 Masters and shot a 59 to win the Bob Hope Classic. This man sets some seriously high standards for himself. What Duval saw is that he needed to become a more athletic specimen to continue to compete with Tiger Woods, who had eclipsed him as the world's No. 1 player.

At the beginning of his career, Duval was more concerned about shedding his reputation as someone who couldn't finish a tournament. Duval had been a highly-decorated college player at Georgia Tech—he was a first-team All-American four straight years, and even led the PGA Tour's BellSouth Classic through three rounds when he was a senior—but he missed in his first try at Q-school. After a successful season on the Nike Tour, Duval joined the PGA Tour, where he immediately finished 11th on the money list in his first season. But over the next 86 tournaments, Duval finished second seven times and third another four, setting off speculation that he wasn't a finisher. At the end of 1997, though, Duval exploded, winning three tournaments in a row—two of them in play-offs—to surge to second on the money list. He won four more times the next season, including the NEC World Series of Golf. It appeared that Duval was ready to solidify his position as Woods' main challenger when he systematically demolished the field at the 2001 British Open to win his first major. But instead of coming out of that experience with more confidence, Duval lost his way. He struggled to set new goals, and hurt his back during training. By 2003, he was struggling to break 75. Still, Duval is too talented to write off. He is working with David Leadbetter to try to regain his old form.

1   2   3   4

When Duval shot his final-round 59 to win the 1999 Bob Hope Classic, he didn't have to make a putt longer than 12 feet. He eagled the 18th hole from ten feet to win the tournament by one shot.

DUVAL'S SWING HAS BEEN BUILT FOR POWER EVER SINCE HE WAS a junior. His father, Bob Duval, a long-time PGA teaching professional who now plays on the Senior Tour, encouraged him to place his left hand on the grip where it was comfortable—in a strong position—then fit his right hand to the left. The strong grip reduces forearm rotation, which also gives the younger Duval more control. The big drives come from Duval's superb body coordination during the swing.

"David's power comes from the torque he creates by having a big shoulder turn," said Bob Duval. "His shoulders turn almost 90 degrees more than his hips, and he keeps that angle right through impact. He doesn't rotate his arms much or have much wrist action. Instead, he swings with the body." And notice how Duval doesn't freeze his head through the swing. Two frames before impact, he's already rotated it toward the target to let his shoulders pass under freely.

5   6   7   8

1

2

3

4

"David has always been flexible, with good hand-eye coordination—he was an all-star in Little League baseball—and he has good balance, a requirement for the golf swing." Bob Duval

IN FRAMES 5 AND 6, DUVAL DEMONSTRATES where his power and accuracy off the tee come from. In frame 5, he's almost fully released his hips, while the club is still waist high on its way down to impact. His upper body is uncoiling ferociously through impact. To get the most out of that power without spraying shots wildly, all Duval has to do at this point is hold on. In frame 6, he's doing just that. The arms aren't doing anything—no flipping or turning—they just follow the firing of the hips. Duval hits the ball shorter than he did in college (he's still plenty long), but he's much more accurate now. In 2000, he was second on the PGA Tour in total driving, a combination of the driving distance and accuracy categories.

5

6

7

8

Duval is the only player aside from Tiger Woods to be ranked No. 1 in the world since the beginning of 1998.

BECAUSE OF DUVAL'S EXTRA-STRONG GRIP AND WIDE ROTATION, HIS CLUB moves to the outside when he first starts his takeaway. By frame 3, though, he's right on plane, and the clubface is dead square. Compare how far Duval's hips have moved from frame 4 to frame 5. His hands have dropped about a foot, but his hips have moved from closed to the target to open. The hip turn is his first move at the top of the backswing and triggers the downswing. Frame 7 shows Duval in a position common to most power hitters—the club is extending out from below his left shoulder. He has swept through the ball with a flatter arc. He hits his iron shots with a more upright swing.

1

2

3

4

5

6

7

8

WHEN HIS PEERS GOT A LOOK AT STEVE ELKINGTON'S SWING, *they figured it wasn't a question of "if" he would win multiple major championships, but "when." Elkington has won one, the 1995 PGA Championship, but his career has been beset with injuries—an allergic reaction to grass, chronic sinus troubles and a torn ligament inside his hip socket, to name just the most recent. He hasn't played more than 23 events in a season since 1993.*

Steve Elkington

When Elkington has been healthy, he has been one of the most dangerous players on the PGA Tour. He's one of only four players to win the Players Championship twice (1991 and 1997), and he won the Vardon Trophy for lowest scoring average on the PGA Tour in 1995—the year he shot one of the most brilliant rounds in PGA Championship history at Riviera Country Club. Trailing third-round leader Ernie Els by six shots going into Sunday, Elkington shot 64 to get into a play-off with Colin Montgomerie. It ended quickly—Elkington sank a 25-foot birdie putt to win on the first extra hole. Elkington had also won the season-opening Mercedes Championship and finished second at the Memorial and Tour Championship that season. Allergies limited Elkington to only 16 events in 1998, but he started off 1999 the right way, birdieing six consecutive holes to win the Doral-Ryder Open, the second time he had won that event in three years. But 2000 was a disaster—only one top ten, more sinus woes that made him withdraw from the US Open and the hip socket problem that forced him to have surgery the week of the PGA. He recovered in time to play as a captain's choice on the President's Cup team in November, but wasn't back to full speed. At this point in Elkington's career, as he nears 40, it isn't a question of whether he'll be competitive (he's proven he can still win), but whether the grind of rehabilitating himself over and over again—and getting back into tournament form—will become too much?

1

2

3

4

THE HALLMARK OF ELKINGTON'S SWING IS ITS FLUIDITY—

something easier to capture on video than it is in still photographs. But compare the frames of Elkington at address and at impact and you can see some of what admirers mean by it. Aside from some body lean, Elkington is in an almost identical position in both photographs.

You get the sense that he doesn't have to work very hard when he swings to get all the power he needs. "One of the reasons Steve's swing looks so smooth is that his swing is technically sound and efficient," said Alex Mercer, his long-time coach. "A player with a flawed swing, no matter how good his tempo, would never look as graceful as Steve." His positions through the swing are perfect at each step. At the top of the backswing, his head has stayed in the same position it was in at address, yet he's fully coiled, with his back to the target. At the finish, he's balanced, with his weight shifted to the outside of his left heel—fully released, but not out of control.

In a 1995 poll of 100 PGA and LPGA tour players, Elkington's swing was voted the best. "Steve's swing is beautiful," said **Nick Price**. *"It's very simple, no-frills, efficient."*

5

6

7

8

COMPARE EACH FRAME THROUGH-
out the swing and you'll see that
Elkington's body angle stays constant
throughout. He doesn't have to make
any extra adjustments to get the club on
plane—he simply delivers it through the
impact zone. Look how similar frames 3
and 5 are. The club is on the exact same
plane on the way to the top as it is on
the way down. His impact position is so
relaxed, it looks like he could have posed
for this photo. In fact, he hit it 285 yards
down the fairway. At finish, he has his
belt buckle facing the target, the sign
of a full, smooth release.

*"Because he trusts his motion, all Steve has to
worry about is swinging the club back and
through as smoothly as possible."*

Alex Mercer, *Elkington's long-time coach.*

1

2

3

4

5

6

7

8

1

2

3

4

BECAUSE HE HAS LONG ARMS, ELKINGTON STANDS A LITTLE
bit further from the ball than other tall players. But his arms are still
hanging loosely from his shoulders—he's not stretching them out artificially.
At the top of his backswing, the club is in perfect position—pointing
directly at the target—and the clubface is square. He can't help but hit a
straight shot from here. Again, notice how relaxed he looks at impact. He's
in a virtually identical position compared to his setup. After impact, the
club is still on the same plane as it was halfway down. Check it with a ruler.

5

6

7

8

*In his first victory, the 1990 Kmart
Greater Greensboro Classic, Elkington
shot a final-round 66 to come from seven
strokes behind.*

WHEN ERNIE ELS WON HIS FIRST US OPEN IN 1994 AT AGE 24, *he was hailed as a prototype for the next generation of championship golfers—a tall (6-foot-3), strong athlete with a gorgeous swing who can hit both 300-yard tee shots and delicate chips with equal dexterity. Els won his second US Open three years later. Now, he's being tabbed as one of the most likely challengers (with David Duval and Phil Mickelson) to Tiger Woods' recent dominance.*

Ernie Els

Els grew up in South Africa excelling effortlessly in tennis as well as golf. He didn't concentrate on golf alone until his early teenage years. The first sign that he could do great things in the game came when he was 16 and traveled to San Diego and beat Phil Mickelson on his home course to win the Optimist Junior World Title.

Instead of staying in America to hone his game in a college program, he turned pro right after high school and joined the South African tour. In 1992, he became the second man to win the Open, Masters and PGA Championships of South Africa in the same year. Gary Player was the first.

When Els beat Colin Montgomerie and Loren Roberts in an 18-hole play-off to win the 1994 US Open, he was still a member of the European Tour, but he began playing almost full-time in America shortly after.

By 1997, he had fully established himself as a multi-national star, playing a full calendar of PGA Tour events and a handful in both his native South Africa and Europe. Els birdied the 17th hole in the final round to take a one-shot lead at the 1997 US Open—it was a lead he didn't relinquish. He was the first foreign-born player to win the Open twice in almost 100 years.

When Els won the 2002 British Open—and then won five times around the world before the 2003 US Open—he proved he was the player best-equipped to challenge Tiger Woods for the title of world's greatest player.

1

2

3

4

Since players not born in the US or Europe aren't eligible to play in the Ryder Cup, Els has had to take his match play frustrations out somewhere else. He won three consecutive World Match Play Championships from 1994–96 and went a combined 6-2-2 in the first two President's Cups.

THE MOST STRIKING THING ABOUT ELS' SWING IS THAT HE DIDN'T HAVE ANY serious coaching when he was growing up. He discovered his natural, flowing swing himself, and has avoided any really invasive changes through his entire career. Instead, he works out specific problems with David Leadbetter, who says that Els is so successful because his swing is so simple. If Els does struggle, it's usually because he hunches over at address. Here, he's in perfect position—balanced, with his arms hanging naturally. Els says he focuses mainly on upper body rotation in the backswing. "The key is making a full shoulder turn," he says. "I like to feel as if my upper body is a coiled spring." Leadbetter describes Els' position at the top of the backswing as perfect—his shoulders have completely turned and his back faces the target, yet his lower body has barely moved. Most players don't have that kind of flexibility. He builds terrific coil against that stable lower body and unleashes all his power against a firm left leg. It's no wonder he hits the ball so far with so little apparent effort.

5

6

7

8

1

2

3

4

Els has finished in the top seven at the US Open four times. In 2000, he tied for second (he was second in three of the four majors that year), but was 15 shots behind Tiger Woods.

FROM THIS ANGLE, YOU CAN SEE HOW FAR AWAY THE clubhead moves from Els' body before he starts his shoulder turn (frame 2). His plane is a little steep in image 3, but he swings so precisely and with such economy of motion that it doesn't hurt him. You can see in frame 5 that his angle of attack is identical to that of his backswing in the same position. At impact, it's clear just how much Els braces against his left side and slings the clubhead through the ball. Part of the reason he looks so fluid and graceful is because he stays in perfect balance throughout the swing. Nowhere is this more apparent than at the finish. He looks like he could stay in that position all day.

5

6

7

8

1

2

3

4

IF ELS STARTS TO SPRAY THE BALL, IT'S BECAUSE

he's doing what you see in frame 4. Here, his club is slightly laid off at the top—it points to the left of the target instead of right at it. From this position, Els has to manipulate his hands to get the clubhead square at impact. If his timing is good, he can save the shot. If he fires his hands too late or too early, he'll either leave the shot to the right or hook it to the left. His steep angle of attack also accentuates any extra hand action because the club spends so little time sweeping through the impact zone. You can see a little extra bow in his right wrist just past impact, a sign that he's given this shot a little extra hand action.

Els won events on at least two tours for seven consecutive seasons going into 2000. He has won eight PGA Tour titles, ten in South Africa, 13 in Europe and one in Japan.

5

6

7

8

IN 1985, NICK FALDO BECAME MORE FAMOUS
*for what he was doing at the practice range than what he did out on the course
itself. Demonstrating a drive for perfection that would come to epitomize him as
a champion, Faldo decided to tear apart the swing that had made him the best
player in Europe and rebuild it into one that would win major championships.*

Nick Faldo

9

It took a year and a half of constant work with teacher David Leadbetter, but in July of 1987, Faldo won the first of his six major championships, the British Open. "The great thing about Nick was that he really committed himself to the changes," Leadbetter said. "That took a lot of guts for someone in his position."

Before the changes, Faldo had been a good player on the European Tour. In 1984, he won five times and was first on the Order of Merit, but he knew that his loose, sometimes unreliable, swing wasn't going to stand up to the pressures of major championship play. After the changes, he became the undisputed best golfer in the world. Along with the 1987 Open title, Faldo won claret jugs in '90 and '93 and green jackets

at Augusta in 1989, '90 and '96.

The '96 Masters victory was a perfect microcosm of Faldo's career. He had never been as popular as Greg Norman, who led by six shots going into that final round. Nor had he been blessed with the set of physical skills that Norman possessed. But Faldo was a relentless pursuer who didn't make mistakes. When Norman started to falter, Faldo took advantage, making meticulous pars when he had to and attacking pins when given the chance. Faldo's spotless final-round 67 gave him his sixth major championship, and his heartfelt embrace of the shell-shocked Norman on the final green went a long way toward softening the harsh image many fans had of this intensely introspective and self-critical man.

1

2

3

4

HERE YOU CAN SEE THE RESULTS OF THAT YEAR AND A HALF OF work. Before the changes, Faldo had a much narrower stance, his swing was much more upright and he had both a prominent leg slide and a lot of hand action through impact. Faldo is now much wider at address, which provides a more stable and less-cramped posture and eliminates that slide. Another major change was the adoption of an early set. Faldo cocks his wrists early in the backswing—you can see it starting to happen in frame 2—and then lets the big muscles of his torso complete the turn. The result is a more compact, flat swing that produces lower, shorter, and more accurate shots. Faldo is a big man, 6-foot-3 and 200 pounds, but he hasn't been especially long since the swing changes. He'll trade that length for the accuracy he gets, anytime. At impact, notice how straight the line is from Faldo's left shoulder down the shaft of the club. Perfect.

Faldo didn't start playing golf until 14—very late by professional standards. He saw Jack Nicklaus playing on television and was inspired. Six years later, he was the European Tour rookie of the year and a member of the Ryder Cup team.

5

6

7

8

1

2

3

4

FALDO IS NO LONGER HUNCHED OVER AT ADDRESS, AS HE was before the changes. Here, he has perfect, balanced posture. In frame 2, you can see the major difference between a professional and the average amateur. Faldo's clubhead is still in front of him. At this point, most amateurs have taken the club dramatically back inside. In frame 3, Faldo has completely turned into his backswing, but his feet are still flat on the ground. Many players lift the left heel slightly at this point to get a little extra turn. Faldo doesn't want any extraneous motion to disrupt his precise swing.

Faldo has won more points (25) and played in more matches (46) than anyone else in the history of the Ryder Cup. He was a member of every Ryder Cup team between 1977 and 1997.

5

6

7

8

1

2

3

4

FALDO'S ADDRESS POSITION IS THE PERFECT PICTURE OF neutrality. His shoulders, hips and arms are all square to the target, and his right arm completely obscures his left. If his grip was stronger, you'd see his left arm peeking out above the right. Throughout the swing, Faldo's spine angle and head position haven't changed at all. He keeps himself in balance and in control. This isn't the way to hit the longest tee shots, but it's a great way to hit every fairway.

"I've been close in a couple of British Opens, but haven't been able to finish the job. The problem is my technique, or lack of it."

Nick Faldo, *shortly before retooling his swing with David Leadbetter.*

5

6

7

8

ONE FACT TELLS YOU ALL YOU NEED TO KNOW

about Raymond Floyd's competitiveness. By the time the 1993 Ryder Cup came around, Floyd was in his second season on the Senior Tour, but Tom Watson picked him as a captain's choice anyway. Floyd made Watson look like a prophet by beating Jose Maria Olazabal—who was three years old when Floyd played in his first Ryder Cup in 1969—2-up to clinch the cup for the Americans.

Raymond Floyd

Floyd's unorthodox swing has been one of the most reliable in the game since the mid-1960s, and he's used it—along with stone cold nerves under pressure—to build impressive credentials. Early in his career, Floyd was known as a partier who wasn't getting the most from his talent. He won twice in his first three seasons, but wasn't consistent enough to crack the top 30 in earnings. Floyd's first major, the 1969 PGA Championship, lifted him to sixth on the money list, but five straight years without a win followed. Getting married in 1973 seemed to calm him down. Right away his play improved. In 1975, he won the Kemper Open and finished 13th on the money list. He destroyed the field at the 1976 Masters, setting the course record in the process. Ten more wins would follow between 1977 and 1982,

including his second PGA Championship win in 1982 at Southern Hills. And just when people thought his career on the regular tour was starting to wind down, he surprised everyone by shooing a final round 66 at Shinnecock Hills to win the 1986 US Open at age 43. In 1992, Floyd became the first man to win events on both the PGA Tour (the Doral-Ryder Open) and the Senior Tour (the GTE North Classic) in the same season. That year, he finished 13th on the PGA Tour money list and 14th on the Senior Tour list, despite playing in only seven senior events. He's been a regular winner on the senior circuit ever since. In 2000, he won his 14th senior title and fourth senior major, the Senior Players Championship. Only Sam Snead has had a similar record for competitive longevity.

1

2

3

4

Floyd and Sam Snead are the only two players to win PGA Tour events in four different decades. Floyd did it in the 1960s, 70s, 80s and 90s. Snead's wins came in the 1930s, 40s, 50s and 60s.

BEFORE JIM FURYK WAS AROUND TO HAVE THE PGA

Tour's strangest swing, Ray Floyd held the title for at least 20 years. Floyd's swing is a series of loops and compensations, but it has served him well. The loops are easier to see in the next sequence, down the line. From this angle, Floyd's position in frame 5 is certainly unique. He has cocked his left knee significantly back toward the ball while straightening his left leg. With his hip turn, it looks like Floyd is about to tip toward the target in a reverse pivot. In the next frame, however, Floyd is in textbook position. Look at the change in both legs. The left one has straightened, while the right is in a more conventional bent position.

5

6

7

8

1

2

3

4

When Floyd won the 2000 Senior Players' Championship at age 57, he was the oldest player ever to win a senior major.

FROM THIS ANGLE, YOU CAN SEE JUST HOW MUCH

Floyd sweeps the club back from the target line. In frame 4, he has the club much further behind him than most tour-caliber players. The kicked-in left knee is even more obvious here, in frame 6, than it was in the face-on sequence. Frame 6 also shows just how flexible Floyd still is, even into his Senior Tour career. In order to compensate for the unorthodox swing path and straight right leg, Floyd must coil his shoulders dramatically at the top. He does, and in frame 7, he's in perfect impact position.

5

6

7

8

FROM THE MOMENT TIGER WOODS TURNED PRO, *he has been the center of attention in every event in which he's played— except one. At the 1999 PGA Championship, Sergio Garcia stole the hearts of the crowd at Medinah with his charisma and go-for-broke style. Just that once, Woods looked like the tired veteran holding on for dear life.*

Sergio Garcia

Woods wound up beating Garcia by a shot, but the most memorable moment at that tournament wasn't Woods making a short par putt to clinch the victory, but Garcia's mad sprint up the 16th fairway after slicing an impossible shot off a tree root and onto the green. Garcia's lack of pretence instantly endeared him to fans everywhere. Here was a kid who didn't hide his feelings—good or bad. He said things other pros only thought about, but never expressed. Golf suddenly looked a lot more exciting.

The 1999 season was a whirlwind for Garcia. He turned pro in April after playing in nearly 30 tour events as an amateur to test himself. He quickly proved he had made the right decision, winning his sixth professional start, the Murphy's Irish Open. Garcia earned enough in that short span to vault onto the Ryder Cup team. At Brookline, Garcia won 3½ points and went

undefeated through foursomes and fourballs with partner Jesper Parnevik.

Garcia's second year as a professional was a little more turbulent. He played full schedules in both the US and Europe and didn't win on either side of the Atlantic. The only consolation was a $1 million check for winning the prime-time "Battle of Bighorn" against Woods late in the year. Critics seemed ready to write Garcia off as an also-ran at age 21, but failed to keep in mind one fact: Garcia was contending for a major championship at an age when Woods was still going to class at Stanford. "Of all the recent young phenoms, Sergio Garcia is the most advanced I've ever seen playing the game—that is, understanding different shots, managing them and controlling his game," said *Golf Digest* teaching professional Hank Haney. He won his first US tour title at the 2001 Colonial.

1

2

3

4

GARCIA ISN'T VERY BIG, ONLY 5-FOOT-10 AND 160 POUNDS,
so his set up and swing are designed to get him more power and distance. In the address photo, his grip is a little stronger than average and he has an aggressive tilt to his shoulders—designed to deliver a powerful upward swipe at the ball. His big speed producer comes at the top of the backswing. He makes a very quick transition from backswing to downswing, which forces the clubhead to lag behind his hands. Frame 4 clearly shows this incredible wrist cock and lag—we compare Garcia's lag to Ben Hogan's on page 183. The swings are similar. The danger here is that this much lag is hard to control. Garcia constantly fights either hooking shots or blocking them to the right because the lag has either released too soon or too late. In the next frame, Garcia's hands are waist high in the downswing, yet the club is still back behind his head. Compare that to the position a classic swinger like Payne Stewart is in, and the difference is tremendous. Look how far the club travels from frame 5 to frame 6. That lag creates an incredible whipping action—a huge power source. Garcia is the longest player for his size on any tour.

Garcia's father, a teaching professional, got him started in the game when he was three. By age 12, Garcia was the club champion.

5

6

7

8

GARCIA SETS UP WITH HIS HANDS LOWER THAN STANDARD.

This position makes it easier to cock his wrists as much as he does at the top of his backswing. Garcia gets into another Hoganesque position in frame 5. He bends slightly at the waist, from where he was at address, to keep the shaft on plane with all the wrist cock. In frame 6, Garcia has fully cleared his hips as he gets to impact—a full release of all the coil created between his upper and lower body. This is another power move. Despite all the whipping around, he's still nice and balanced at the finish.

As an amateur, Garcia's career match-play record was 32-1. His only loss came in the 1998 US Amateur, to Hank Kuehne.

1

5

2

6

3

7

4

8

1

2

THE MOST INTERESTING FRAME IN THIS SEQUENCE IS NUMBER
4—you can see how fast Garcia changes direction at the top of the
backswing by the amount of flex he's putting on the shaft. If he didn't use
an extra stiff shaft in his driver, the club would flex out of control. In the
next frame, you can really see how Garcia starts to squat a little bit on the
way to impact—another Hogan move. He makes an extemely full finish,
with the club coiling all the way around his neck and pointing back at the
target again. That's common for players trying to get the most distance
they can. He's generated so much speed that he needs extra time to put a
brake on it at the end.

"You can't teach experience,
but Garcia already has a feel for the game."

Golf Digest *teaching professional* **Hank Haney**.

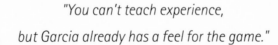

3

4

5

6

7

8

FOR WALTER HAGEN, GOLF WAS A MEANS TO AN END.
He was an entertainer and a competitor. Golf was just the medium. When Hagen played an event or an exhibition, it was a spectacle. He would often arrive at the first tee minutes before his time—sometimes in a limousine—and make a great show of changing his shoes. He'd carelessly hit his first shot, smoke a cigarette and make the crowd howl with laughter over one of his jokes.

Walter Hagen

He'd hit loose shots, then cut his opponent's heart out with a cold-blooded recovery. Hagen almost single-handedly raised the status of the touring pro, and his colorful quotes generated the publicity the fledgling professional tour needed. And his playing record? Hagen won 11 major championships along the way—including four consecutive PGA Championships (1924-27).

Hagen got into the game as a caddie in his hometown of Rochester, and developed into a fine player. But he was an equally good baseball pitcher, and considered signing a professional contract for that sport. But his play at the 1913 US Open—Hagen finished fourth while amateur Francis Ouimet was shocking established British players Harry Vardon and Ted Ray to win the title—convinced him golf was his game. He dedicated himself to practice, and the next year, he won the US Open at age 21. World

War I limited the number of tournaments that were being held, so Hagen hit the road and played in exhibitions, picking up fees for his appearances and often making more on side bets with local pros. He became an experienced head-to-head player, psyching his opponents out with both gamesmanship and clutch shots from seemingly impossible spots. In Hagen's era, the PGA Championship was contested at match play—a format perfectly designed for Hagen. He won his first in 1921, then reeled off four straight from 1924 to 1927.

By the late 1920s, Bobby Jones had eclipsed Hagen as the game's biggest star, but Hagen continued to make a lucrative living playing exhibitions, even after he faded from competitive golf in his late 30s. He must have caused quite a stir in the small towns his caravan of three limousines visited throughout the 1930s and 40s. And Hagen loved to create a stir.

1

2

In 1926, Hagen beat Bobby Jones, who would go on to win both the US and British Opens that year, 12-and-11 in a special 72-hole exhibition.

3

4

HAGEN HAD A LONG, LOOSE SWING that was based mostly on feel. He sprayed shots with his driver and long irons, but was an exceptional short-iron player. More importantly, he was terrific under pressure. He had the confidence to try high-risk shots and pulled them off when he had to. Hagen had a noticeable sway in his backswing, and his left arm bent at the top (frame 2). As a result, he didn't bring the club through impact consistently if his timing was off. But Hagen's head did remain relatively still through the swing. He wasn't the wild slasher everyone made him out to be—more like a modern-day Seve Ballesteros, complete with the match-play game face.

BEN HOGAN DIDN'T HAVE THE PHOTOGENIC, CHARISMATIC QUALITIES *of a Tiger Woods. He didn't play in golf's television era, which started just after his stretch of domination. He was simply the best player of his era. His peers knew it, and the fans came to know it by what they saw. That was good enough for Hogan.*

Ben Hogan

He never wanted the limelight anyway. But winning four US Opens, two Masters, two PGA Championships and one British Open (and winning three of those titles in one year, 1953), tends to draw some attention. Hogan had a relentless desire to perfect his golf swing and eliminate a hook that had blighted him since he was a kid. The result—the most reliable swing of any professional in the game's history.

From 1940 to 1942, Hogan won 15 tournaments, but his first major didn't come until 1946. At that point, he was considered a nice player, but not one that would go out and prove he was the greatest champion in the game. Hogan won 13 tournaments in that '46 season, then seven more in 1947. In 1948, he won his first US Open, and set the tournament scoring record in the process. But early in 1949, Hogan's career and life hung in the balance when his car was hit head on by a bus as he drove between tour stops. He broke a multitude of bones, and blood clots formed in his shattered legs, that guaranteed Hogan would never walk without discomfort for the rest of his life. His competitive career was probably over. But by 1950 was back playing. At the '50 US Open, he made it into a playoff with Lloyd Mangrum and George Fazio and shot a 69 on pure guts to complete his comeback. Hogan was forced to drastically reduce his schedule because of his weakened legs—he would play less than ten events, focusing on the majors and tournaments near his Texas home. In 1953, Hogan had his season for the ages. He broke the Masters scoring record by five shots, then won the US Open by six shots. Hogan then decided to make his first trip to the British Open, and shot a course-record 68 in the final round to win by four. Hogan had played in six tournaments that year and won five. The British Open would be Hogan's last major.

1

2

3

4

5

6

8

8

ONE OF THE COMMON
descriptions of Hogan's swing is that it seemed like it was nine-tenths over when he addressed the ball. The action was just a foregone conclusion. Hogan set up with a neutral grip and his back very straight. His lower body stayed relatively quiet throughout the downswing, but he made a tremendous turn with his shoulders, coiling and building up lots of power. Frame 4 is classic Hogan. His left arm is ramrod straight, and you could hang laundry on his club shaft. Hogan had some hip turn through impact, but not nearly as much as modern players like Tiger Woods or David Duval. His power came from the lag he shows in frame 6. The clubhead is still behind his head while his hands are waist high. And impact? Perfect precision.

"Hogan had to hit three practice balls for every one Nicklaus hit. He was the most dedicated practicer of all time. His tenacity had no equal."

Paul Runyan

EVERY SPORT HAS ITS ULTIMATE ACCOMPLISHMENT.

Mark McGwire's 70-home run season. Wilt Chamberlain's 100-point game in basketball. Wayne Gretzky's 92 goals in a hockey season. In golf, Bobby Jones' 1930 season has survived as the single greatest in the game's history, and the ultimate measuring stick for any future champion.

Bobby Jones

Jones won each of the four tournaments that were then considered major championships—the US Amateur and Open and the British Amateur and Open.

After sweeping through the British Amateur, British Open and US Open, Jones finished his slam in a style befitting such a champion. He won his semi-final match against Jess Sweetster 9 and 8, then beat Gene Homans 8 and 7. For all the drama that surrounded his march through the four majors, he didn't leave much doubt when he finished it off.

Jones captured not just the sports headlines with his achievement, but the attention of the world at large. He was feted with a ticker-tape parade in New York City and memorialized in magazines, books and even a film—a California movie production company paid him handsomely to make a series of short movies about his golf swing.

Jones was the dominant golfer of

his era, so winning any of those events wasn't much of a surprise. But to play at such a high level over the course of all four is something only two men have ever come close to matching in the more than 70 years that followed—Ben Hogan in 1953 and Tiger Woods in 2000. And after Jones accomplished this remarkable feat, he made sure nothing would ever tarnish it. He retired immediately after, aged 28, and at the pinnacle of his career.

Along with his sparkling playing record, Jones' great legacy is the creation of Augusta National and the Masters tournament. Jones proudly oversaw the tournament until his death from syringomyelia, a crippling disease of the spine, in 1971. It had been more than 40 years since his glory days on the course, but Jones' star hadn't dimmed in the slightest. He is remembered as both a champion and a gentleman.

1

2

3

4

In the nine-year stretch between 1922 and 1930, Bobby Jones finished first or second in the US Open eight times.

JONES' SWING WAS LONG AND GRACEFUL—BOTH

because Jones was a terrific athlete and because he understood the physics of hickory-shafted clubs. Any violent or abrupt move in the swing would cause the hickory shaft to torque out of control. So Jones made a flowing move through the ball to take advantage of the whipping action of the wood without losing control of the clubhead. Jones' swing actually looks fairly modern, even with the old clubs. In frame 4, he makes a big hip turn—so much so that his left foot comes almost all the way off the ground—so that he can make an easy and gentle transition to the downswing. Like most great ball strikers, his head remains very still throughout the swing. After impact, Jones keeps his arms extended until they reach shoulder-height, which takes a lot of strength.

5

6

7

8

IF HOLLYWOOD HAD WRITTEN A SCRIPT *about a 5-foot-8 guy in Coke-bottle glasses making good on the PGA Tour— making so good that for six years, he was leading career money earner—it would be too fantastic even for the movies. But Tom Kite has been a success at every level, getting more out of his small frame than anyone ever thought possible.*

Tom Kite

He shared the 1972 NCAA title with University of Texas teammate Ben Crenshaw. He was 1973 PGA Tour rookie of the year. He grinded out 19 victories in 27 seasons on the PGA Tour and he won his own personal holy grail, the 1992 US Open at Pebble Beach. Now, he's a consistent winner on the Senior Tour, where he's already won a major, the 2000 Tradition. Not bad for a kid who couldn't see the ball land if he didn't have his glasses on.

Kite was never the flashiest player on tour. Crenshaw attracted more attention when he turned pro, a year after Kite, with his golden hair and big smile. And when Crenshaw won the first PGA Tour event he ever played as a professional, he overshadowed his old teammate even more. Throughout the late 1970s and through the 1980s, Tom Kite was never the best player on the PGA Tour, but he was always in the group of three or four guys who had good years. He led the tour in

earnings only twice, in 1981 and 1989, but finished lower than 20th in earnings only twice between 1974 and 1994. He made cut after cut and was competitive every week. Kite didn't drive it as long as the tour's biggest hitters. He made his money from 100 yards in. The first pro to carry a third wedge, Kite was perfectly happy to rely on his short game to threaten in tournaments in which par was a good score. He got his ultimate chance at the 1992 US Open. Kite's final-round 72 at Pebble Beach in gale-force winds was one of the finest rounds ever played, and it gave him a two-shot victory over Jeff Sluman.

Technology finally caught up with the guy who spent more time on the range than anyone since Ben Hogan when he moved to the Senior Tour. After LASIK eye surgery, Kite could finally see the ball hit the green without help from those big glasses. He likes what he sees.

1

2

3

4

KITE HAS ALWAYS BEEN WILLING TO TINKER WITH HIS SWING
to improve his results. And unlike most other players who make changes, it
doesn't take Kite very long to assimilate them. His record attests to that
consistency: from 1974 to 1987, he went without a win in only four of
those seasons. Like Nick Faldo, Kite's priority is accuracy over distance. He's
made some adjustments over the years to gain a few yards—most notably
the stronger grip, the increased shoulder tilt at address and the
exaggerated wrist cock halfway through the downswing, but his goal is to
bring the club through impact on line. In the impact photo here (frame 6),
Kite is in perfect position, with the shaft in line with his left arm and his
head well behind the ball. "Tommy has the rare ability to be able to listen
to a wide assortment of advice, sort through it, select what works for him
and discard the rest," said his long-time teacher, Harvey Penick.

*Kite was the first PGA Tour player to reach the $6
million, $7 million, $8 million and $9 million plateaus
in career earnings. He's since made more than $2
million on the Senior Tour.*

5

6

7

8

1

2

3

4

KITE KEEPS HIS HIPS RELATIVELY STILL COMPARED TO HIS
shoulders, which he turns aggressively. He barely turns his hips at all in the
first three frames, but in frame 4, he's got his back to the target. Kite
excercises extensively on flexibility machines to be able to keep that turn.
These photos were taken shortly after he won the US Open in 1992, but he
looks the same now on the Senior Tour. After impact, in frame 7, Kite has
fully extended his arms. He gets the most out of the swing that he can. His
finish position, complete with the panama hat, is distinctive. You can tell
it's him from two fairways away.

Kite played on seven Ryder Cup teams
(1979–89, 1993) and was the captain
of the 1997 team.

5

6

7

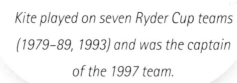

8

1

5

2

6

3

7

4

8

KITE IS A LITTLE BIT UPRIGHT AT ADDRESS, UNCOMMON FOR A shorter player. That upright stance helps him wind his shoulders so much further than his hips, which is clear in frame 3. You can tell from the wrinkles in his pants that he's creating exceptional coil. One thing common to all good golf swings is the position of the right elbow in frame 5. Kite's is in perfect position—glued to his side. If the elbow comes off the hip there, it's impossible to get full extension—and maximum power. This is the best angle to see just how well Tom delivers the club town the target line.

"One of the things that makes golf so fascinating is that you never stop learning. Every time you play or practice you pick up something new." Tom Kite.

THE YIPS HAVE CLAIMED MANY VICTIMS.
Sam Snead was plagued with them throughout his career. Ben Hogan suffered so badly on the greens that he said putting shouldn't even be part of the game. Put a big net on the green and make players hit into it to score, Hogan said. Johnny Miller won't play on the Senior Tour because his putting stroke is so shaky. That makes what Bernhard Langer has been able to accomplish all the more impressive.

Bernhard Langer

Langer has beaten back severe yips at least four different times in his career with a variety of putting strokes, putters and putting grips. That he's been competitive for 20 years on the European Tour is proof enough of his tenacity, but Langer has gone a step further. He's won the world's most demanding putting contest, the greens at Augusta National and the Masters—twice.

Langer's first struggle with the yips came in his earliest years as a professional. He worked relentlessly on his iron play to offset his problems with the putter. When his putting stroke finally came back, he was ready to capitalize. He won for the first time as a professional in 1980, at the Dunlop Masters, then didn't stop for 15 years. In addition to the two green

jackets he won at Augusta in 1985 and 1993, he has won 37 times in Europe. His last four European wins came after yet another battle with the yips. Langer cobbled together a strange "claw" putting grip and used a long putter to get his stroke back.

When the Great Britain and Ireland Ryder Cup team grew to include all of Europe, Langer, a German, became a fixture along with his Spanish counterparts, Seve Ballesteros and Jose Maria Olazabal. In 1985 and 1987, he helped Europe to win and retain the cup, triumphs that helped dull the pain he must have felt after missing a six-foot putt that would have won the cup for Europe at Kiawah Island in 1991. That miss was just another psycological hurdle Langer cleared with grace.

1 2 3

"The most important thing (at Augusta) is to hit good iron shots into the right positions so you have easier putts."

Bernhard Langer *on the secret to playing well at Augusta.*

LIKE OTHER SMALLER PLAYERS, LANGER HAS ALWAYS

looked for more distance. It was even more true when he was growing up. "I was quite small, but I still wanted to hit the ball far," Langer said. "So I developed a very strong grip to hook the ball and make it go farther." He hasn't moved away from that grip, even today. "If he tried to change, he would lose rhythm, power, and much worse, the trust he has in himself," said Langer's long-time coach, Willi Hoffman. Langer avoids hooking by pulling aggressively with his left hand through impact, bringing the grip through just before the clubhead. In fact, all the pieces work very well together. Langer is one of the premier long-iron and fairway wood players in the game.

4 5 6

IF TOM LEHMAN'S CAREER ENDED TOMORROW, *he'd look back fondly on his triumph at the 1996 British Open, but he wouldn't be able to shake the feeling that he missed his chance at the US Open. Only one player besides Lehman has ever led the US Open after three rounds for three consecutive years. Bobby Jones did it from 1928 to 1930, but he won two of those three tournaments. Lehman came up empty each time.*

Tom Lehman

But even if it remains Lehman's destiny to win only one major in his career, the fact he was able to fight his way back to the PGA Tour at all and be a success there, after three years in minitour purgatory, is a testament to his tenacity.

By the end of the 1985 season, Lehman didn't know if he belonged on the PGA Tour. He had lost his card for three consecutive years, never finishing higher than 158th on the money list. He drifted to Asia and South Africa, played in satellite events there, and then came back to the PGA Tour's version of the minor leagues—the Ben Hogan Tour. There, he found a new lease of life, winning four times in two seasons and earning another crack at the big leagues in 1992. He

didn't waste his second chance. In 1994, Lehman won the Memorial, Jack Nicklaus' tournament, and was second to Jose Maria Olazabal at the Masters. He won the Colonial, Ben Hogan's tournament, in 1995, and was in the top 15 on the money list for a second consecutive season. But 1996 was his greatest year to date. At Royal Lytham & St Annes, Lehman shot a course-record 64 in the third round, then held on with a 73 in the final round to beat Ernie Els and Mark McCumber by two shots and win his first major championship. At the end of the season, he won the Tour Championship by six shots, and locked up the season money title in the process to cap a memorable year. He's still looking to recapture that dominance.

1

2

3

4

"THERE'S A TENDENCY TO PAY TOO MUCH ATTENTION TO WHAT the body is doing during the swing and to forget where the club is," said *Golf Digest* teaching professional, Hank Haney. "At certain key stages of the swing, it's important that the shaft be parallel to the plane line it was on at address. Tom's ability to do that makes his swing a good one for the average player to copy." Lehman does some idiosyncratic things in his swing, like driving his hips toward the target more than turning them, but, as Haney said, Lehman keeps the club on plane throughout. Another unique element in Lehman's swing is how narrow he sets his feet at address. He likes to play the ball from right to left, and the shoulder-width stance he takes when hitting the driver helps him to make a bigger body turn on the backswing and swing the club through from the inside. At the top of the backswing, Lehman doesn't cock his wrists very much, but the narrow stance has enabled his left shoulder to get behind the ball—a power position if ever there was one. Compare the top-of-the-backswing frame to the next one and you can really see that hip slide.

Lehman set a PGA Tour single-season record when he earned $1,780,159 in 1996. He was also named the Tour's player of the year.

5

6

7

8

1

ONE OF THE HARDEST PLACES TO KEEP THE CLUB ON PLANE IS at the point when the club stops moving along the ground and starts to make its way upward. Most average players bring the club quickly inside, which usually results in an over-the-top move and a slice. In frame 2, Lehman has kept the club perfectly on plane. Lehman has a thick chest and shoulders, so he doesn't worry as much about hip turn and a backswing that passes parallel at the top. He relies more on his arm strength and leg drive to get his distance. Compare frames 4 and 6. Lehman uses a lot of leg action to drive through the shot. His left leg is firm at impact, but it isn't straight.

5

2

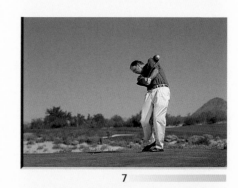

6

3

7

4

"Tom's swing positions are, for the most part, neutral, meaning it takes only a small adjustment to tailor a shot to fit any situation."

Hank Haney, *on Tom Lehman.*

8

1

2

3

4

WHAT SETS LEHMAN'S SWING APART FROM THOSE OF OTHER

professionals is the move he makes as the club comes through the downswing. Lehman dips his knees and gets into a significantly lower position than he was in at address—a lot like Byron Nelson used to. He doesn't "pop up" until well after the ball is gone, and the club is wrapping around his body in the finish. This dip move helps Lehman keep his head significantly behind the ball at impact, while his arms swing through, whipping through impact against his firm left side. Add in the fact that Lehman hits a low draw off the tee and it's easy to see how he gets as much distance as he needs.

In his first three seasons on the PGA Tour,
Lehman made only $39,477.
After playing minitours for three seasons,
he came back and won $579,093 in his
fourth PGA Tour season.

5

6

7

8

JUSTIN LEONARD STARTED PLAYING UNDER THE WATCHFUL EYE
*of Randy Smith at Royal Oaks Country Club in Dallas. Even at age ten, the small
and slight Leonard couldn't carry the ball more than 130 yards with his driver. In
junior tournaments, he often couldn't reach longer par-fours in two shots.
Despite those disadvantages, he used his course management skills to beat kids
who could hit it 30 yards past him off the tee.*

Justin Leonard

"It sounds odd to say, but Justin Leonard today is pretty much the same golfer as the ten-year-old kid who came to me for lessons back in 1983," said Smith, a *Golf Digest* teaching professional. "Then, as now, he was a mature thinker who beat the opposition with smart course management, patience, concentration, discipline and by playing the game one shot at a time."

As the stakes got higher, Leonard continued to flourish. He was a two-time All-American at the University of Texas, and was the first player ever to win four consecutive conference tournaments. He won the 1992 US Amateur and was a member of the victorious Walker Cup team the next season. When he graduated from Texas in 1994, Leonard didn't want to wait until late October to go to PGA Tour Q School. Instead, he played ten events on sponsor's exemptions with hopes of winning enough money to earn his

card the hard way. He did it, and hasn't looked back. Since that first season, Leonard hasn't finished any lower than 22nd on the money list. His greatest victory came at the 1997 British Open. Trailing by five shots going into the final round, Leonard proceeded to shoot a 65 to win by three shots over Jesper Parnevik and Darren Clarke. He reinforced his reputation as a comeback kid early in 1998, when he rallied from another five-shot deficit to win the Players Championship. But the most dramatic finish of them all came at the 1999 Ryder Cup. Leonard had struggled all week, failing to win a point going into Sunday's singles. His poor play continued early in his match with Jose Maria Olazabal, and Leonard quickly fell four down. But he rallied to get back into the match, then sank the putt that was heard around the world; a 45-foot bomb on the 17th, to ensure a halve and an American victory.

1

2

3

4

In order to get into position to earn the half point that decided the 1999 Ryder Cup in his match against Jose Maria Olazabal, Leonard had to come back from 4-down. He did it by winning holes 12 through 15.

LIKE OTHER GOLFERS WHO AREN'T BLESSED WITH A LOT OF

size, Leonard (who runs only 5-foot-9 and 160 pounds) does what he can to get more distance. He uses a slightly stronger grip, and he makes an aggressive turn in his backswing. Like Tom Lehman, he gets his head behind his left knee at the top, but Leonard is more flexible, and gets the club past parallel. He has also stayed nicely in balance—as much as he's turned, he hasn't moved outside his right leg. There has been no sliding. Leonard retains his wrist cock long into the downswing, then releases all of that energy into the ball. "Justin is 'stacked up' perfectly at impact," said Randy Smith. "His upper body is directly over his rear end, which is over his right knee, and his left knee is directly over his left foot. There is no wasted energy." Leonard's finish is classic—he's facing just left of the target and the club has wrapped all the way around and across his right shoulder.

5

6

7

8

"Justin's strong suits are balance, sound fundamentals and performing within his capabilities."

Golf Digest *teaching professional* Randy Smith.

LEONARD'S TAKEAWAY IS ONE-PIECE. HE doesn't do anything with his hands. His body turn is what starts the club back in the backswing. Frame 4 shows how perfectly Leonard has set the club at the top. The clubhead is pointing directly at the camera, like the sight on a rifle. As he makes his way through the downswing, Leonard fires his hips aggressively. They're already open by the time the clubhead is halfway down. He's creating a slingshot effect, with the club cracking like a whip at impact. At the finish, Leonard's zipper faces the target, but his momentum has carried his chest and shoulders past that—they point well left of the target.

1

2

3

4

5

6

7

8

1

2

3

4

LEONARD WAS 30 YARDS SHORTER THAN

the kids he competed against in junior golf, but he
never gave in to the temptation of overswinging to try
to get more distance. He has tried to get longer, but he's
done it within the context of his solid swing mechanics. He stays
balanced throughout the swing, with no lunging or any other wasted motion.
This is especially evident at the finish, where he's fully released, balanced and
relaxed. "You'd have to give him a good push to knock him over," said Smith.

*When Leonard won the British Open in
1997 at age 25, he was the second
youngest ever to do it. Seve Ballesteros
was 22 when he won in 1979.*

5

6

7

8

WITH A NAME LIKE HIS, DAVIS LOVE III OUGHT TO HAVE A RICH
golf pedigree—and he does. Love's father, Davis Love Jr, was one of the preeminent instructors in the game and a great player in his own right. Love Jr introduced his son to golf at an early age and was active in helping him to develop his game to tour level.

Davis Love

Love had never had instruction from anyone else until he was forced to—his father was killed in a plane crash in 1988. Regrettably, the senior Love never got a chance to see his son win the title teaching professionals hold the most dear, the PGA Championship in 1997.

Love grew up in the game, and he never had any doubt he would follow in his father's footsteps as a teacher or tour pro. He played college golf at the University of North Carolina, where his biggest claim to fame might have come from introducing another Tar Heel, basketball player Michael Jordan, to the game. Love turned pro in 1985 and made it through Q-school on his first try. He's been a staple on tour ever since. Love's father got to see him win his first professional event, the

1987 MCI Heritage Classic, but was gone by the time Love had his best season in 1992, winning three times and finishing third on the money list. Along with Phil Mickelson and Colin Montgomerie, Love had been collared with the "Best Player Without a Major" tag througout the early 1990s. Mickelson and Montgomerie are still searching for their first majors, but Love dropped out of the group with a dominating performance at Winged Foot in 1997. He went 66-66 on the weekend to beat Justin Leonard by five shots and win the PGA. As he walked up the 18th hole with his brother Mark, who was caddieing for him, the persistent rain that had been falling stopped and a rainbow appeared on the horizon. It was the perfect ending to a perfect tournament.

1

2

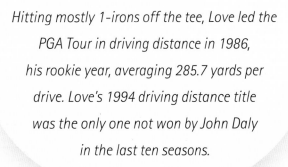

3

4

LOVE SWINGS THE CLUB LIKE SOMEONE WHO HAS HAD GOOD
coaching since the beginning, and he has. From the time he started in the game, his father, Davis Love Jr, impressed on him the importance of building a swing with good fundamentals. In these sequence photographs, there are no extra or compensating moves—just a pure, powerful swing. Love has a very athletic set up at address. He's in a slight crouch, like the one a shortstop gets into just before the ball is pitched. His knees are flexed and his arms are extended, but Love doesn't over-reach for the ball, which would cause tension. Frame 3 is one of the main reasons Love hits the ball such a long way. The larger an arc a player can create on the backswing, the more time he has to wind up and create speed on the downswing. Love gets his hands—and the club—incredibly far away from his body on the backswing. Jack Nicklaus and Tiger Woods are the only other two players who get the club in a position like this. He couples this wide takeaway with great lag on the downswing, shown in frame 5. By the time he reaches impact, he has everything lined up—his head, left arm and shaft.

Hitting mostly 1-irons off the tee, Love led the PGA Tour in driving distance in 1986, his rookie year, averaging 285.7 yards per drive. Love's 1994 driving distance title was the only one not won by John Daly in the last ten seasons.

5

6

7

8

1

2

3

4

IN FRAME 1, YOU CAN SEE HOW LOVE SETS UP WITH THE BALL at the heel of the club. He does this to promote an inside-to-out swing path, which produces a draw. He sweeps the club back from the ball in the next frame without lifting it at all. At the top of the backswing, Love demonstrates just how flexible he is—he gets the club past parallel, but he barely lifts his left heel off the ground. Love says he swings at 85 percent of capacity at most. He feels he gets more distance on a consistent basis hitting the ball squarely with slightly reduced power than he would swinging full tilt and missing the sweet spot on the club. That's great advice for the average player to heed—sometimes less is more.

Love has won one major, but has come close a number of other times. He has four other top-four finishes in majors—two each at The Masters and the US Open. He also finished in the top ten at the British Open every year from 1997 to 1999.

5

6

7

8

1

2

3

4

FROM THIS ANGLE, IT'S EASIER TO SEE JUST HOW MUCH
Love stretches when he takes the club back. In frame 3, he's trying to get the club as far away from his body as possible without losing his balance. At the top of the backswing, he hasn't done anything to manipulate the club. His left wrist is still nice and flat. At impact, Love is in textbook position—his hips have cleared before his shoulders and his head hasn't moved. In fact, his head stays in a perfect position until the last frame, when the swing is over and the ball is long gone.

"We wanted the body to follow the swing and the turn be a natural result of your bones being connected together, not twisted into some unnatural position. Davis Love III has the classic modern golf swing."

Harvey Penick.

5

6

7

8

AS PRECOCIOUS AS TIGER WOODS WAS BY WINNING TWICE *in his first eight events as a pro, even he didn't burst onto the PGA Tour scene in the style Phil Mickelson arrived. Mickelson was a junior at Arizona State when he won the Northern Telecom Open in 1991 as an amateur after getting into the field on a sponsor's exemption.*

Phil Mickelson

He was in the midst of a college golf career in which he won a US Amateur, NCAA individual title and was named a first-team All-American four times. Until Woods turned pro in 1996, Mickelson was the most heralded player to turn pro since Jack Nicklaus in the early 1960s.

The wins came quickly—two in 1993, four in 1996 and another four in 2000. Nobody would dispute that Mickelson has had a fine career to this point. He was closing in on 20 career wins during the 2001 season, and has finished in the top 15 on the PGA Tour money list in five of his eight full seasons. But Mickelson's spectacular talent has also made him a target for criticism from those who think he hasn't achieved enough. A second-

place finish—by a single stroke—to Payne Stewart at the 1999 US Open is as close as Mickelson has come to winning a major championship, the standard by which golf champions are measured. Mickelson says he wouldn't be disappointed if he retired without winning a major, but he burns with a visible competitiveness when he's in contention in regular tour events.

He's also one of the few pros around today who doesn't shrink from an on-course confrontation with Woods. He beat Woods head to head at the 2000 Buick Invitational. So Mickelson has to be a favorite every time he tees it up at a major championship, but it also adds to the pressure of fulfilling those lofty expectations.

| 1 | 2 | 3 | 4 |

Golf is the only thing Phil Mickelson does left-handed. He writes, throws, eats and bowls righty. His father played right handed, so Mickelson faced him and followed along lefty. Johnny Miller and Ben Hogan developed the opposite way—left-handed in everything but golf.

MICKELSON BUILT HIS SWING FROM THE HOLE BACKWARD, inventing creative short shots at the practice green and bunker in the back yard of his parents' San Diego home, then graduating first to executive length, then to full-sized courses. He's always been known more for his work around the greens than for his full swing, and when he struggles, it's usually because his big, flowing swing has gotten a little loose. It's easy to see in the sequences here how much of a feel player Mickelson is. He isn't in classic positions anywhere except for the one place it matters—at impact. His address position is too upright and stiff, and he turns his hips too aggressively early in the backswing. "The golf ball doesn't know that Mickelson's legs start too straight, or that his hips turn too much, or that his left arm folds too much at the top. All it knows is impact, and Phil is in great position when the club meets the ball," said *Golf Digest* teaching professional, Hank Johnson. In the last year, Mickelson has softened some of these idiosyncrasies by working with *Golf Digest* teaching professional, Rick Smith. His swing is tighter, and as a result Mickelson is longer and more accurate off the tee.

| 5 | 6 | 7 | 8 |

1

2

3

4

ONE OF THE THINGS SMITH HAS BEEN WORKING

on with Mickelson is improving the position Phil is in in frame 4. Mickelson's left leg has straightened at the top of the backswing, which lets his hips over-rotate. He loses coil, which costs him power. Smith has created more of a differential between Mickelson's hip and shoulder turns, recreating the coil. Mickelson has always been in good position at impact. Here, his hips have cleared (his belt buckle has gone past the ball) as his shoulders get to square. Mickelson's incredible timing and feel let him get away with a less-than-perfect technique.

In 2000, Mickelson finished third in the PGA Tour's All-Around ranking despite being ranked 125th in driving accuracy. He was in the top five in five other categories—scoring average, driving distance, putting average, eagles and birdies.

5

6

7

8

THE TWO MOST STRIKING FRAMES IN THIS
sequence are numbers 3 and 4. In frame 3,
Mickelson has moved his club to a plane flatter
than the one it was on at address—the club
now points outside the ball. From there, he lets
his left elbow fold dramatically at the top,
which gets his hands far behind his head. To
hit solid shots from here, Mickelson has to have
great tempo, because his hands need time to get
out from behind his head before they can move
straight down toward impact. He makes the
transition perfectly, and halfway down, he's
back on plane.

*Not only can Mickelson hit an
amazing collection of trick shots—his most
spectacular is a flop shot he hits back over his
head from an uphill lie—he isn't afraid to hit
them in competition. He routinely used a lob
wedge to hit flop shots from ultra-tight grass at
the 1999 US Open at Pinehurst, when most of the
field was using the bump and run.*

1

2

3

4

5

6

7

8

1

2

3

4

MICKELSON'S TRADEMARK SHOT IS THE FLOP, WHICH HE'S
willing to hit from any lie. It's a great shot for the average player to have
in his or her bag as well, but only under certain conditions—when the flag
is tucked closely behind some obstacle, when the green is too fast for a
chip to stop near the hole, or when the ball is sitting down in grass and
solid contact with a chipping stroke would be difficult.

"This shot is more forgiving than many conventional shots, provided
you follow three simple rules," said Mickelson. The right kind of sand
wedge is critical—one with 60 degrees of loft and bounce near the rear of
the clubhead, so it can slide through turf instead of bounce off it.

Reading the lie is the next critical element. The club could slide right
under the ball if it's sitting up on the grass. Tempo is the third key—don't
try to accelerate the club through impact. To hit it, Mickelson places the
ball off his front instep and sets up with the club laying completely open,
with the back of it on the ground. He cocks his wrists sharply, then, from
the top, lets gravity do the work.

Mickelson starts with his stance open, but the face of the club is
pointed at the target. Like a bunker shot, he hits about an inch behind the
ball and keeps the clubface open well past impact. "It explodes off a cushion
of grass and turf," Mickelson said. "You rely on the trajectory of the ball
[almost straight up] to stop it near the hole, not backspin." This shot does
take a larger swing, because the ball has to fly high to get to the target.
Mickelson lets the momentum of the swing take him to a full, free finish.

The tempo for this shot is slow and gentle, not rushed and aggressive.
Since Mickelson cocks his wrists early in the swing, he doesn't have to
worry about them after that point. He simply takes the club to the top,
then brings his hands down with the wrists still cocked. The swing plane is
very steep, and the wrists stay cocked long into the downswing. You can
see the small patch of turf behind the ball explode as the ball leaves the
club. Aside from the open stance, Mickelson here looks just as he would in
his finish after an iron shot.

5

6

7

8

FOR A SHORT TIME, JOHNNY MILLER HIT THE GOLF BALL AS WELL AS *anyone who has ever played the game. For a span in the early 1970s, Miller was as good as anyone has ever been. Injuries, putting problems and a commitment to his family kept Miller from seriously challenging Nicklaus, Trevino and Watson, but ask any of those players which man they'd least like to see chasing them during that decade and they'd all most likely answer Johnny Miller.*

Johnny Miller

The first glimpse of what Miller could do came in 1973, in the final round of the US Open at Oakmont. Miller had been a middle-of-the-pack player before that, winning two tournaments in his three-plus seasons on tour. But at Oakmont, it all came together.

Miller shot a 63—the lowest score ever recorded in a major. He hit every green in regulation and even missed several short putts that could have given him an even better round.

Regardless, it was enough to beat John Schlee by five shots and give Miller his first major. He didn't give his opponents a chance to catch a breath. Miller won the first three events of the 1974 season and played his first 23 rounds under par. He went on to win eight tournaments that year and set the money record with more than $350,000 in earnings. Miller started 1975 by winning the Phoenix Open by 14 shots, then taking the Tucson Open the next week by nine. Miller struggled

with his putting throughout his pro career, but had hit the ball close enough to the flag to offset it. By the time he got to the 1976 British Open, he had painted a red mark on the top of his putter grip with nail polish and was focusing on that during the stroke. It worked well enough to give Miller his second and last major at Royal Birkdale, by six shots over Jack Nicklaus and Seve Ballesteros.

Miller never regained his top form after Birkdale. He won events every year from 1980 to 1984, but never seriously challenged in a major. He reduced his schedule to become a broadcaster and only played in a few events. But twice, Miller came down from the booth to win the Pebble Beach National Pro-Am—in 1987 and 1994. Bad knees and a lucrative deal from NBC have kept him from playing in many Senior Tour events, but, even in his mid-50s, he can still strike the ball as well as he did in the mid-1970s.

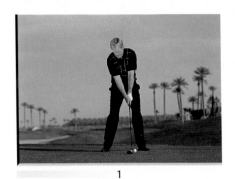
1

2

3

4

Of Miller's 24 PGA Tour wins, 14 came out west. He won the Tucson Open four times, the Pebble Beach National Pro-Am three times and the Phoenix Open twice.

MILLER'S FATHER WAS INSTRUMENTAL IN BUILDING THE fundamentally sound swing you see here. Miller never saw a golf course until he had grooved his swing, hitting into a tarp from a mat in his garage. By the time he was ten years old, he had developed the pure iron swing that he kept throughout his career. Miller is naturally left-handed, and he uses his dominant left side to great effect in his swing. He starts with a neutral grip—the palms face each other and are perpendicular to the ground—and his hands are low and close to his body. His arms are hanging loosely from his shoulders, without too much tension. The major difference between Miller's swing—one that is built for accuracy—and Jack Nicklaus', which is built for power, is in the setting of the wrist cock in the backswing. Miller sets his wrists early, in frame 2, while Nicklaus keeps his wrists uncocked longer to create a wider swing arc. Miller keeps this early wrist cock consistently through the rest of the backswing—which makes him very stable at the top—and keeps it until his hands reach waist height in the downswing. Then, they uncock naturally and the clubface comes through square.

5

6

7

8

1

2

3

4

Miller was the first player to be inducted into the World Golf Hall of Fame in 1996 at the World Golf Village in St Augustine, Florida.

THESE PHOTOGRAPHS WERE TAKEN WHEN MILLER was in his late 40s. Even then, he was still flexible enough to make a very full backswing. His finish is the signature position of the 1970s player. He's in a "reverse C," with his head and shoulders tilted to the left. Modern players like Tiger Woods and Karrie Webb finish in a much more upright position, with the shoulders centered over the the hips. A look at the shaft position in this frame (8) can also tell a lot about what kind of shot a player has just hit. Miller's shaft is in a more horizontal position, which signifies a fade. A higher, more vertical shaft position at finish indicates that the player has probably hit a draw.

5

6

7

8

1

2

3

4

Miller finished tied for eighth at the 1966 US Open as an amateur. It was played that year at Olympic, the course he grew up playing in San Francisco. Miller, a sophomore at Brigham Young University at the time, had planned to caddie at the tournament for extra money, but made it through qualifying to get into the field.

FRAME 4 SHOWS WHY MILLER IS SO ACCURATE.

If the club shaft bisects the space between the right and left forearms when the hands reach waist height on the downswing, it translates into a perfect plane and swing path. If it covers the right arm, the player will hit a draw or push the shot to the right. If it covers the left arm, the player has come over the top and will either slice or hit a pull to the left. Miller's shaft is in perfect position. Frame 4 shows how Miller's left knee initiates the downswing. His left arm follows, pulling the club through to impact. The wrists are forced to uncock because of centrifugal force, not because of a conscious effort.

5

6

7

8

COLIN MONTGOMERIE'S CAREER CAN BE DESCRIBED *in two ways. First, he was Europe's steadiest player throughout the 1990s, ranking first on the money list seven times in a row—from 1993 to 1999—and winning more than 20 events. He's been the rock of Europe's Ryder Cup team, playing in every match since 1991 and anchoring both the victorious 1995 and 1997 teams.*

Colin Montgomerie

Conversely, Montgomerie has never won a major championship, and his scowling visage on the course has never endeared him to American fans. He has taken more abuse than is fair from them and, because of it, has promised that he'll never play more than a few events on the US Tour.

Montgomerie's golf pedigree is unmatched by almost any other player. His father was the secretary of Royal Troon, a British Open venue, and Montgomerie excelled as a player from the time he was small. He won both the Scottish Stroke Play (in 1985) and the Scottish Amateur (in 1987), then came to the US to play college golf at Houston Baptist University.

Montgomerie turned pro in 1987 and immediately earned his playing card at Q-school. He's been a fixture ever since. His first European Tour win came at the 1991 Scandinavian Masters. The next season, 1992, would be the last Monty was anything but

number one until the end of the decade. His best season to date came in 1999, when he tied the European Tour record with six wins and broke the single-season earnings record. But he would trade many of those accolades to have another crack at the three major-championship close calls that went against him. In 1994, Ernie Els beat him and Loren Roberts in an 18-hole play-off for the US Open at Oakmont. Montgomerie made it into a play-off again at the 1995 PGA, but Steve Elkington sank a long birdie putt to win. Montgomerie also had a chance to tie for the lead with a birdie at the 1997 US Open, but he missed the putt. Els went on to win that one, too. So Montgomerie is lumped together with Phil Mickelson as one of the best players never to have won a major—even though that single omission overshadows a record unmatched in Europe for its consistency over almost a decade.

22

1

2

3

4

MONTGOMERIE'S SETUP AND BACKSWING ARE UNIQUE. AT address, he has his hands significantly behind the ball and from there, he drags the club back very low to the ground. In frame 3, Montgomerie has shifted his upper body significantly to the right as he starts his shoulder turn. The danger here is moving from this position to a reverse pivot, where the shoulders fall forward in the backswing, then pitch backward through impact. Monty keeps his head in a consistent position and moves into a good turn. His head actually gets in the way of his shoulder turn in frame 4—his left shoulder bangs into his chin when he reaches the top of the backswing. Frames 5 and 6 are perfect—he unwinds well, and at impact, his head is well behind the ball and his left arm is perfectly straight. His finish position has that recognizable tilt and high hand position.

Montgomerie is the first player ever to win the Volvo PGA Championship three consecutive years, from 1998 to 2000.

5

6

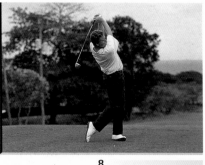

7

8

1

2

3

4

MONTGOMERIE PRIZES ACCURACY MUCH MORE THAN

distance, so he does everything he can to hit the ball squarely, rather than try to hit it hard. Like the other great ball strikers we've shown here (Duval, Trevino, Parnevik), Montgomerie closes the clubface slightly on the way back—it's most noticeable in frame 2. He also redirects the club from a very steep backswing plane to a flatter plane on the downswing, just like Trevino. You can see the transition his body makes from frame 4 to frame 5. Montgomerie's upper body goes from tilting toward the target to tilting slightly away—putting his head behind the ball.

Montgomerie was the European Player of the Year four times in five years between 1995 and 1999. He's won that award more than any other European player.

5

6

7

8

1

2

3

4

5

6

7

8

IN FRAME 2, MONTGOMERIE IS CONTINUING TO EXTEND THE club away from his body without any wrist cock. From here, it moves into a very upright position, with just a hint of a wrist cock. He doesn't fully set his hands until the top of the backswing, in frame 4, when the club moves significantly past parallel. Montgomerie is a stocky player, but he is surprisingly flexible. At finish, he's in a form of the "reverse C" position that was so popular in the 1970s. Montgomerie's head stays back a little bit more than it would in the finish of a "90s" swing. He puts a little more pressure on his lower back because of it.

Montgomerie is undefeated in his Ryder Cup singles career, with a record of 3-0-2.

"ALL YOU CAN DO IS BEAT THE PLAYERS THEY PUT IN FRONT OF YOU."

Byron Nelson says those words more than 50 years after he had one of the single greatest seasons in the history of the game. He won 11 consecutive tournaments in 1945 and won the only major championship played that year, the PGA. Only three other seasons come close to matching it—Bobby Jones in 1930, Ben Hogan in 1953 and Tiger Woods in 2000.

Byron Nelson

Most of the debate rages about the quality of competition Nelson faced in 1945. World War II was in full tilt, and the likes of Ben Hogan weren't playing because of military service.

It's impossible to speculate how Nelson would have done against a full compliment of challengers. Regardless, Nelson was one of the purest ball-strikers in the history of the game, and his record can stand on its own merits.

That Nelson was able to accomplish so much in 1945 wasn't a total surprise. He had won the 1937 and 1942 Masters and the 1939 and 1942 US Opens. The year before, 1944, he had won eight tournaments, the money title and recorded the first scoring average below 70 in the history of the professional tour.

But in 1945, he found a whole new level. In the 120 rounds he played, he averaged 68.33 strokes per round—the best of all time until Woods went lower still in 2000. And while Hogan wasn't playing much golf in 1945, Sam Snead was, as was Jug McSpaden and Lloyd Mangrum. Nelson beat them all during that 11 tournament stretch. He won the All-American Open by 11 shots and broke the tour scoring record with a 259 at Seattle. But by 1946, Nelson had grown tired of the stress and attention that came with all of the records he had been setting. He won another six events that season, but after the PGA Championship, he announced his retirement. He moved back to Fort Worth to a ranch he had purchased. He was only 34 years old, but his stomach couldn't take it anymore.

1

2

3

4

From 1944 to 1946, Nelson went 113 consecutive tournaments without missing a cut. His 18-win season in 1945 earned him $63,335 in war bonds.

BYRON NELSON IS CALLED THE FATHER OF THE MODERN GOLF
swing. Some of that had to do with timing. Nelson was a member of the first generation of golfers who played with steel-shafted clubs. Steel was more consistent and torqued less than hickory, and enabled players to make a more athletic and powerful move through impact. Nelson was the first to incorporate the new equipment successfully into his game. His stance was much more upright, and he held his wrist cock much longer into the downswing than either Bobby Jones or Walter Hagen could with hickory. Nelson also finished his swing in an upright position, with his head centered over his left foot. He looked a lot like tour players do today in this position. The combination of his precise action and new equipment made Nelson one of the most accurate iron players of all time. At the Masters, he hit the stick with an approach and the ball bounced into the water—one of the four times that round he had hit the pin with an iron shot.

5

6

7

8

JACK NICKLAUS HAS BEEN THE GIANT IN THE GAME SINCE HE BEAT *Arnold Palmer in an 18-hole play-off to win the 1962 US Open in his rookie season. He won 18 professional majors, finished second in another 19 and spent 17 consecutive seasons in the top ten on the PGA Tour's money list. But the true testament to Nicklaus' greatness might be that in his prime years, from 1962 to 1979, he finished in the top 10 in almost 70 percent of the events he played in.*

Jack Nicklaus

One of the reasons Tiger Woods is so celebrated for his achievements today is that nobody has done anything like it since Nicklaus in the early 1960s. In between winning two amateur titles, Nicklaus finished second to Arnold Palmer in the 1960 US Open—as an amateur. Ben Hogan, who was paired with Nicklaus in the final round, knew just how good the stocky kid from Ohio could be. He said Nicklaus could have won the Open "if he had a brain in his head." Nicklaus did just that in his rookie year, winning at Oakmont.

In his second season, he won two more majors—the Masters and the PGA, then completed the career Grand Slam in 1966 by winning the British Open. Only five men have done it, and only Woods did it quicker.

Nicklaus' best season might have been 1972, when he won the Masters and US Opens by three shots apiece, then vied for the British Open title before finishing second. Tom Watson

eclipsed Nicklaus as the game's dominant player in the late 1970s, but Nicklaus was still a force in major championships, winning the 1978 British Open at St Andrews, the 1980 US Open and PGA Championship and the 1986 Masters. "When you got down to the end with Jack, you knew you had to win it," said Johnny Miller, one of Nicklaus' contemporaries. ".He never made a mistake, and that was the perfect style for major championships."

Nicklaus still plays senior golf, but concentrates most of his energy on his mammoth golf course design operation. He says he doesn't believe in "ceremonial golf," and will quit playing competitively the moment he doesn't think he has a chance to win. That he can still make a run at winning the Masters late in his 50s, like 1998, when he shot a final-round 68 to finish tied for sixth, shows just how formidable Jack Nicklaus was and on his day, still is.

1

2

3

4

IN HIS TIME, NICKLAUS HAD THE MOST POWERFUL SWING THE game had ever seen. With the inferior equipment and weaker-lofted clubs of the mid-1960s, Nicklaus was still hitting middle-iron second shots into the par fives on Augusta's back nine. Like more modern big hitters, Nicklaus started his power generation with a wide arc, as you can see in the frame 2. He got (and still gets, as you see here) incredible extension away from his body on the backswing. Nicklaus' first teacher, Jack Grout, always encouraged him to hit the ball as hard as he could and to worry about direction later. So Nicklaus has always tried to turn as much as he could—you can see it in the stretch wrinkles on the side of his shirt at the top of his backswing—and to get the club high and behind him at the top of the backswing. That's difficult to do once you reach your 50s, but Nicklaus has excercised feverishly to try to keep himself as flexible as possible. His swing still resembles the one he had when he was 30 years old, even if he doesn't have the strength he once did.

Nicklaus was named Sports Illustrated*'s Athlete of the Decade for the 1970s, a span in which he won eight major championships, five money titles and five PGA Player of the Year awards.*

5

6

7

8

1

2

3

4

FROM HERE, YOU CAN SEE HOW NICKLAUS EXTENDS HIS ARMS at address and remains in a very balanced position. He makes an upright backswing, which means he'll have to re-route the club onto a flatter plane in the downswing. In frame 5, you can see that he's done this successfully— the butt of the club points right at the ball. Nicklaus has always reached impact with his head far behind the ball—a power position that also promotes high, soaring shots with both woods and irons. "I call it the 'dinosaur swing,' because golfers who keep their heads that far behind the ball are almost extinct," says Johnny Miller. "That's one reason he hits it so high, but it's also the reason his back hurts him."

"He plays a game with which I'm not familiar."

Bobby Jones, *on Jack Nicklaus winning the Masters by nine shots in 1965.*

5

6

7

8

1

2

3

4

5

6

7

8

Eight of Nicklaus' ten wins on the Senior Tour have come in senior major championships, including the 1991 and 1993 US Senior Opens.

FROM THIS ANGLE, IT'S EASIEST TO SEE THE TRADEMARK OF Nicklaus' swing: the flying right elbow in frame 4. Nicklaus has had this idiosyncratic move from the very beginning, when he was trying to hit every ball out of sight as a kid on the range at Scioto Country Club in Columbus, Ohio. Nicklaus has always been stocky, with a thick chest and powerful, shortish arms. The move came about out of necessity—if Nicklaus wanted to get his hands that far behind him, he was either going to have to dislocate his shoulder or allow his elbow to stray from next to his chest. Teachers don't advise it, because it promotes a loose motion at the top of the backswing, but Nicklaus' exceptional feel and timing—and the fact that he hit a million balls on the range—let him use it to his advantage.

GREG NORMAN HAS WON MORE THAN 80 TOURNAMENTS WORLDWIDE, *including two British Opens. For a ten-year stretch, he was among the top two or three best players in the world. He has parlayed his good looks and business sense into a $250 million clothing, golf course design, ship building, wine making and turf producing empire. He is one of the five most-recognizable golfers on the planet.*

Greg Norman

But when the book is closed on Greg Norman's playing career, critics will be quick to emphasize all the things Norman didn't do, rather than all the achievements. Norman won a bushel of Australian events, then started playing part time on the European Tour. By the time he started his PGA Tour career in 1984, Norman had already won 26 Australian and European events.

Almost immediately after he started playing in America, Norman started playing well enough to get himself into contention in almost every major championship. A theme started to develop right away. Pick a way for a tournament to be lost—taken away by somebody else's spectacular shot, given away by a single bad swing or simply bad luck—and Greg Norman experienced it. In 1986, Norman led all four majors after three rounds, but won only the British Open with Bob Tway holing a bunker shot at the last

to win the PGA championship. At the 1989 British Open, Mark Calcavecchia beat him in a four-hole play-off after Norman hit it into a bunker that had never been reached before from the tee. Norman faltered on Sunday's back nine and let Corey Pavin pass him to win the 1995 US Open. The ultimate disappointment came in 1996, at the tournament Norman had most wanted to win.

He led Nick Faldo by a seemingly-insurmountable six shots going into the final round of the Masters, but shot a 78 to give the green jacket to Faldo.

Norman will be hailed for the $10 million in career earnings, the three Vardon Trophies for low scoring average on the PGA Tour and the countless other millions he's earned in business, but his sustained record of great play over 20 years could well be overshadowed by the list of what-could-have-beens and near-misses.

1

2

3

4

Two courses Norman has designed, the TPC at Sugarloaf (BellSouth Classic) and the Great White Course at Doral Resort and Country Club (Genuity Championship), are sites of PGA Tour events.

IN ALL THE NEAR-MISSES GREG NORMAN HAS HAD IN MAJOR championships, it has rarely been his full swing that has let him down. In fact, Johnny Miller calls him the best driver of the golf ball—the combination of length and accuracy—in the history of the game. Because Norman picked up the game so late in life, at age 16, he never had to contend with trying to gain distance. He has always hit the ball very long, and still does now in his mid-40s. He may struggle with finesse shots, but his full swing has always been solid. Norman's most common mistake was to slide his hips rather than to rotate them, which made him lose shots to the right. It was this that cost him a chance at the 1986 Masters. He worked with Butch Harmon in the mid-1990s to fix that flaw, as well as trying to flatten his swing plane and reduce his big backswing. In frame 4, Norman has the club short of parallel, but his left hand is in a better position—the wrist is flat, as it needs to be at impact—plus, he still hits the ball a long way.

5

6

7

8

1

2

3

4

NORMAN'S ADDRESS POSITION IS VERY GOOD.

His knees are centered over the balls of his feet, and his shoulders are over his toes. He also has his hands extended enough to make a wide, power-storing backswing. He takes the club back slightly inside the target line, but he'll copy that on the way down and hit a powerful draw. Shoulder and hip injuries kept Norman out of action in 1998 and 2000, but the surgeries (reconstructive shoulder surgery and arthroscopic hip surgery) actually helped him to get back closer to the swing you see here, which was photographed in 1995, rather than limited him.

Norman has had 19 top-five finishes in the four major championships through 2000. He has finished second eight times.

5

6

7

8

Norman's final round at the 1993 British Open at Royal St Georges is one of the finest in major-championship history. He shot a 64 to catch Nick Faldo and Corey Pavin and win his second major title.

NORMAN MAKES A BIG SHOULDER TURN IN relation to his hip turn. His hips don't show any sign of movement until frame 3, when his shoulders have already turned nearly 90 degrees. At the top of the backswing, the clubface is parallel to the angle created by his left forearm—a perfect position. In the next frame, Norman keeps the club in great position, with the shaft pointing directly at the target line. His finish position is classic Norman—the club resting on his neck, right foot up on its toe. Even without the signature wide-brimmed hat, you can tell it's him.

1

2

3

4

5

6

7

8

MOE NORMAN WAS BLESSED WITH SOME OF THE MOST IMPRESSIVE
*hand-eye coordination the game has ever seen. But throughout his prime golf
years, Norman was a virtual recluse—he hated talking to people he didn't know.
Despite being able to hit the ball pure enough to be able to delcare that he was
going to roll a drive over a narrow footbridge 240 yards away and then do just
that, he was perpetually insecure about his strange-looking swing.*

Moe Norman

Galleries laughed at his strange action, and considered him something of a sideshow. So Norman never made an impact on the PGA Tour, but his record in amateur and professional events in his native Canada prove that he is one of the most accomplished ball-strikers in the history of the game.

Norman was a shy kid with a high voice and big ears—so he was the object of a lot of teasing. He kept to himself, and beating balls at the range was a perfect diversion for such a solitary person. When he was 19, in 1948, Norman decided to dedicate one complete summer to perfecting his golf swing at the range near his home in Kitchener, Ontario. Every day, he hit a minimum of 600 balls—wiping his bloody hands on the back of his pants to keep them from slipping on the grip. He never had lessons because he couldn't afford them, but he had plenty of time. By the mid-1950s, Norman

had built a swing that could produce hundreds of perfectly straight shots in a row, and he built himself into one of the dominant amateur players in Canada. He won consecutive Canadian Amateurs, then turned pro in 1958. In 1966, Norman won five of the 12 Canadian PGA Tour events he entered and finished second in five others. But he was so insecure about his swing and his unsophisticated way of dress that a brief attempt, in 1959, was his only foray into American golf. But Norman has always been seemingly unconcerned about anything besides golf, and he was happy to stay in Canada and give exhibitions. After turning 50 in 1979, Norman reeled off seven straight Canadian PGA senior championships, and as recently as 1991, he shot a 59 at age 62. Norman might be a curiosity, but nobody can dispute how well he hàs been able to hit a golf ball.

1

2

3

4

IRONICALLY, THE SWING NORMAN BUILT IN HUNDREDS OF
hours by himself on the practice range has become the model for a golf
instruction system called Natural Golf. People now pay to learn the swing
that was an object of ridicule throughout the 1950s and 1960s. Everything
about Norman's swing is devised to eliminate extra movement. At address,
his feet are spread wide apart, outside his shoulders, and his knees are
locked straight. This wide, stiff stance forces him to make a small,
controlled pivot. Norman also grips the club well into his palms, which
reduces wrist action. Since Norman will hit his drive on the upswing, he
sets up with the club well behind the ball. With that restricted pivot,
Norman's backswing is short and compact. From there, he drives his hips
toward the target. At impact, Norman is, aside from the wide stance, in a
classic position. Notice how the tee has barely budged. Norman once hit 50
drives in a row from the same tee, without having to adjust it. "I hit balls,
not tees," he said.

*"Unusual swings aren't necessarily bad swings. If
you have good balance, you can overcome almost
any swing flaw. The key is to repeat the same swing
every time, which Moe is able to do through
countless hours of practice."*

Golf Digest *teaching professional* **John Elliott**.

5

6

7

8

1

2

3

4

5

6

7

8

AT ADDRESS, NORMAN CERTAINLY DOESN'T LOOK LIKE ANYONE else in this book. His legs are straight and his arms reach out far in front of him for the ball. He's at least a foot farther away from the ball than most other tour players. But in frame 4, Norman has the butt of the club pointing directly at the ball—no matter what kind of mechanics are involved, he keeps the club on plane. At impact, only the slight bend in his right knee is different from where he was at address, and the ball is in the middle of the clubface.

Norman played in only two majors, the 1955 and 1956 Masters. He withdrew after two rounds in 1955 (the cut was after three that year), and missed the cut in 1956.

1

2

3

4

NORMAN'S GRIP IS UNCONVENTIONAL. HE HOLDS THE CLUB IN the palm of his right hand, so that it acts as an extension of his forearm. They act together throughout the swing. With his left hand, he holds the club under the heel pad and across the palm. He doesn't link his hands in any way—no interlock or overlap. All ten fingers are on the club. You get a good look at this grip in frame 2. Norman keeps his upper body remarkably still from frames 1 to 6. Only after the ball has gone does he release into his finish.

Norman once hit 1,540 drives in a seven-hour exhibition. None were shorter than 225 yards, and every one landed in a marked, 30-yard-wide, landing zone.

5

6

7

8

IS IT REALLY ANY SURPRISE THAT THE CORES OF THE GAME'S TWO *legendary Spanish champions—Seve Ballesteros and Jose Maria Olazabal—have games that are nearly identical? Both made their games with feel and touch. If anyone in the world has better hands than Ballesteros, who, with all of his recent struggles, still leads the European Tour in putting, then it might just be Olazabal.*

Jose Maria Olazabal

When Ballesteros could control his propensity for hitting wild tee shots, he was the best player in the world. That was in the early and mid-1980s. Now, Olazabal is in a similar position. He, too, struggles off the tee. But when he's right, as he has been in two impressive wins at the Masters, he's as good as anyone in the world. And that touch!

Olazabal has been groomed for golf greatness from birth. His father, Gaspar, is the greenskeeper at a course in San Sebastian, that opened on the day Jose Maria was born. As a rookie in 1986, he won twice and finished second on the money list. The next year, he was playing with his idol, Ballesteros, in the Ryder Cup at Muirfield Village, where the Europeans won their second cup in a row.

Olazabal and Ballesteros are 11-2-2 as a pair in Ryder Cup play, better than any duo in history. Olazabal has always played most of his golf in Europe, where he has won nearly 20

times, but in the trips he has made to the United States, he usually goes home with something shiny. In 1990, he won the World Series of Golf by ten shots, the PGA Tour record until Tiger Woods' performance at the 2000 US Open. In 1994, he repeated at the World Series, but that win was secondary to his accomplishments at the Masters. Tied with Tom Lehman going into the final round, Olazabal shot a 69 to win by three.

Olazabal's second Masters victory, in 1999, was even more special because of what he had to go through just to be able to play. By the end of the 1995 season, he could barely walk because of rheumatoid arthritis in his feet. After 18 months in bed, thinking his career was over, Olazabal got back on his feet with help from German doctor Heinz-Wilhem Mueller-Wohlfahrt. The Masters win, by two shots over Davis Love, came in only his second full season back.

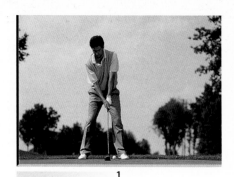   

1   2   3   4

Olazabal turned 35 in 2001, but he's already a veteran of six Ryder Cup teams. The only one he's missed since 1987 was in 1995, when he was out with foot problems.

OLAZABAL'S FULL SWING PLAYS ONLY A SECONDARY ROLE IN HIS
golf game. He uses it to get the ball near the green, and that's where he makes all of his money. Like Ballesteros, Olazabal relies more on feel and flow than technique. When he struggles with his timing, he is exceptionally wild off the tee—something that doesn't get you in as much trouble in the light rough of Augusta National as it does in the jungles that lurk off the fairway at a US Open venue.

Olazabal sets up in an athletic position, with a weak left-hand grip. He makes a sweeping backswing, tilting almost to the point of a reverse pivot at the top. In fact, Olazabal has struggled with reverse pivoting—moving weight forward on the backswing and back on the downswing—during his professional career, a rare problem for an accomplished player. Olazabal's plane is also very steep—great for irons, but more challenging for longer clubs. Olazabal's clubhead only stays in the hitting area for a fraction of the time that it does for someone who sweeps the club through impact, like Lee Trevino.

5   6   7   8

BY THE TIME OLAZABAL HAS MADE IT HALFWAY

In 1994, Olazabal finished seventh on the PGA Tour money list even though he only played eight events in the season. He won two, the Masters and the World Series of Golf, and finished second in another.

through his backswing (frame 3), he's already turned his shoulders almost 90 degrees. Most players don't even do this at the top of their backswing, much less at this position. He actually turns his back even farther at the top, and because of that gets the club way past parallel at the top, so that it starts pointing to the ground again. From there, Olazabal's hands move straight down, which creates tremendous clubhead speed through impact. In frame 6, the clubhead is perfectly square at impact—you can even see all the grooves. Olazabal turns his shoulders completely through the finish—he's actually facing well left of the target when he's done.

1

2

3

4

5

6

7

8

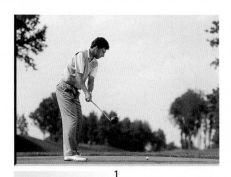
1

2

3

4

Olazabal joined the PGA Tour full-time for the first time in late 2000. Before 2001, he had never played more than 13 American events in a season.

"OLAZABAL HAS A YOUNG MAN'S SWING," SAID *Golf Digest* teaching professional David Leadbetter. "Only someone with the suppleness of youth could coil his torso as much as Jose Maria does." Frame 5 illustrates how much timing is a part of Olazabal's swing. Because he makes such a huge turn, his hips fire toward the target while his shoulders are still closed—they need to go farther than normal because they were turned so far in the opposite direction. If Olazabal's hips clear too quickly, he blocks shots to the right. If they clear quickly and he tries to save the shot with his hands, he often hits a big hook. But when the timing is right, Olazabal is in Davis Love III's league as a long hitter.

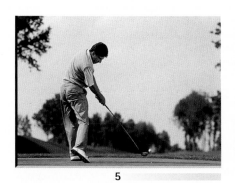
5

6

7

8

ARNOLD PALMER'S INFLUENCE ON GOLF HAS COME FROM MORE *than just tournament results, career money earned or any other kind of statistic. When the game was first televised in the late 1950s, it needed a charismatic star to breathe life into the low-quality, black-and-white pictures. Palmer was just the man for the job. He wore his emotions on his sleeve, his face showing exactly what he was feeling.*

Arnold Palmer

He had an awkward, slashing swing that sometimes looked like a ten-handicapper's. He chain-smoked and constantly pulled up his pants to keep his shirt tucked in. He was the everyman golfer, going full tilt to beat all of the well-groomed, country-club stars at their own game. Of course, winning four Masters titles, two British Opens and a US Open didn't hurt his standing as a legend of the game. His combination of skill and electric charisma made Palmer one of the first mega-rich sports personalities, complete with endorsement deals and corporate tie-ins. He's been the game's most influential spokesman for the last 40 years.

Palmer's father was the working-class superintendant and club professional at the private Latrobe Country Club in Pennsylvania. Palmer could only hit balls at the club when it was near dark and the course was empty, but he took every chance he could get. Palmer won the caddie championship at Latrobe four years running, then played college golf at Wake Forest. After college, Palmer signed up for a three-year hitch in the Coast Guard. While in the service, he kept playing, and won the 1954 US Amateur while stationed in Cleveland. Palmer was 26 when he decided to turn pro—old by today's standards—but he was married and more mature, which contributed to his quick success.

By 1957, he had won six tournaments. Then, in 1958, he won his first major, the Masters. In 1960, Palmer had his greatest season. He won the Masters with birdies on the last two holes to win by a shot from Ken Venturi, then took the US Open by shooting a final-round 65 to come from a seven-shot deficit. Palmer missed winning his third major in a row at the British Open by one shot from Kel Nagle at St Andrews.

1

2

3

4

PALMER'S SWING WAS NEVER RHYTHMIC AND GRACEFUL. PART of his appeal to the masses was that he looked like the everyman when he swung a club. But Palmer was a powerful, accurate driver of the ball in his prime, mostly because of great feel and blacksmith's forearms, which helped him to keep the club on line through brute force. He also kept his head very still throughout the swing, which gave him a consistent pivot point. "You'll rarely see a golfer who turns better with less hint of a sway either coming back or coming through," said Jack Nicklaus about Palmer's swing. But in these photos, Palmer is struggling with a swing that was built for a younger, stronger man. He doesn't turn in the backswing as well as he did, and his famously stable head now bobs back and forth in frames 4, 5 and 6. He still makes good contact because he has great feel, but the consistency isn't there.

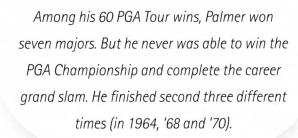

Among his 60 PGA Tour wins, Palmer won seven majors. But he never was able to win the PGA Championship and complete the career grand slam. He finished second three different times (in 1964, '68 and '70).

5

6

7

8

1

PALMER IS HUNCHED OVER AT ADDRESS, WHICH DOESN'T GIVE his arms enough room to work under and through in the downswing. "The vast majority of the time, what you do in your swing is the result of what you've done with your setup," said *Golf Digest* teaching professional Peter Kostis. "Palmer's faulty setup leads to a poor turn that's restricted, and a swing plane that's flatter than would be acceptable." Of course, Palmer was 65 when these were taken, and he shot his age, 71, at the 2001 Bob Hope Classic. Everything is relative.

5

2

6

3

7

4

Palmer has played in 48 Masters, 40 US Opens and 35 British Opens.

8

KARRIE WEBB AND ANNIKA SORENSTAM MAY BE THE PRESENT FOR THE *LPGA, but Grace Park is the future. The talented 20 year-old made one of the most anticipated debuts on the LPGA Tour in years in 2000. She has the talent and charisma to become the LPGA's next star, and seems more willing to accept the limelight that goes with it than the more reticent Webb and Sorenstam.*

Grace Park

Park won everything there was to win in amateur golf. As a freshman at Arizona State, she won the three biggest events in women's amateur golf—the US Amateur, Trans-Amateur and Western Amateur—and helped the Sun Devils to win the 1998 national title. She played five LPGA events as an amateur in 1999, finishing second at the Safeway LPGA Golf Championship and tied for eighth at the US Women's Open. At the Open, she led the field in driving distance by nearly ten yards. Those performances encouraged her to turn pro, which she did right after the Open. Not wanting to wait until LPGA qualifying school, Park started playing on the Futures

Tour right away. Her performance in limited action on the LPGA's developmental tour erased any doubts she might have had that she had made the right decision. Park won five of ten events, was named Futures' player of the year and earned a card for the 2000 LPGA season. A rib injury kept her out of action for more than a month, but Park still won her first LPGA event, the Kathy Ireland Greens.com Classic, and finished 19th on the money list. More than her ability to hit 300-yard drives, what sets Park apart is her confidence. She isn't intimidated by the LPGA's best and should be a force for the next 15 or 20 years.

1

2

3

4

Park won 55 national junior, college and amateur titles from 1992 to 1999. When she swept the three "major" amateur titles in 1998, she was the first to do that since Patty Berg in 1938.

PARK IS AVERAGE SIZE—5-FOOT-6 AND 125 POUNDS—BUT SHE generates incredible clubhead speed. Like the game's other young power hitters, Park gets great extension away from the ball on the backswing and makes a full turn. "She takes it back to the top very smoothly, then cranks it on the way down," said Mike LaBauve, Park's coach and a *Golf Digest* teaching professional. "It isn't a violent move at all—more like the effortless power of Fred Couples and Ernie Els." Park retains her wrist cock long into the downswing, then drives her hips through impact. Look how much more her hips have turned through compared to her shoulders in frame 6. And like Woods, Couples and Els, her head is still well behind the ball.

5

6

7

8

PARK COULD ACTUALLY GET MORE POWER

than she does. She has a big turn, but the differential between the amount she turns her shoulders and the amount she turns her hips isn't as large as it is for other players, but she probably won't fool with things too much. She still can hit it 275 yards without any problem, and her club is in perfect position at the top of the backswing. Why change? In frame 6, she has fully unleashed her hips and shoulders into impact and transmitted all of her power into the ball. When she hits it square, she can carry the ball 300 yards—amazing for someone of her size.

Park was an American Junior Golf Association All-American every year from 1992 to 1997, and was the AJGA's player of the year in 1994 and 1996.

1

2

3

4

5

6

7

8

1

2

3

4

PARK'S MOST COMMON SWING FLAW—A TOO-
upright backswing and too-flat downswing—is noticeable
in this sequence. When she has to re-route the club back
on plane, she has to manipulate her hands, like in frame 7.
"Grace has such good feel about where she is during her
swing than she can make an athletic correction for coming
in too shallow and still hit decent shots, even when she
isn't striking the ball well," said LaBauve. "She was making
the same mistake before her final Futures Tour event [in
1999]. We worked it out on the range the night before the
first round and she won by eight shots."

"Grace's swing is as natural as they come. She has never needed a lot of technical instruction." Mike LaBauve.

5

6

7

8

ON THE PGA TOUR IT TAKES A SWING TO IDENTIFY MOST PLAYERS *from a distance. Not so with Jesper Parnevik, who has won tournaments wearing skin-tight pink pants, hip-hugging purple plaid pants or a canary yellow shirt. His caps come built with the brim snapped upward. He keeps patent leather manufacturers busy with his golf shoe orders. But underneath all of the flash is one of the game's most powerful iron players—and one of its rising stars.*

Jesper Parnevik

The first attention Parnevik received on the international scene was the kind he probably wouldn't have preferred. Parnevik was leading the 1994 British Open by two when he played the last hole, but his career-long aversion to looking at on-course scoreboards hurt him. Thinking he needed a birdie to win, he played the hole too aggressively and made a bogey. Nick Price finished eagle-birdie-par to win the title by one shot.

By 1997, Parnevik was a four-time winner on the European Tour, and far more established as a pro. Still, the British Open eluded him. This time, Justin Leonard shot a final-round 65 to catch him on Sunday.

Now, Parnevik is getting attention for both his sense of style and his play.

He won his first PGA Tour event in 1998, the Phoenix Open, and broke into the top ten in earnings in 2000.

Parnevik's play for Europe in the Ryder Cup has been even more impressive. He and Sergio Garcia were unbeaten as a team in the 1999 matches, and those two men, along with Colin Montgomerie, were the core point-getters for the European side that came up just short. Parnevik's next challenge is to break through and win a major championship. His game is well-suited for the British Open, where length and the ability to keep the ball low under the wind are prized traits. He has been a regular contender there, and has to be considered one of the tournament favorites regardless of the venue.

1

2

3

4

PARNEVIK EARNS HIS MONEY WITH HIS IRON PLAY—HE'S ONE of the longest and most accurate iron players on the PGA Tour. "He takes a club with plenty of loft and then tends to deloft the club through impact, hitting down on the ball," said *Golf Digest* teaching professional, Peter Kostis. "Most average players don't hit down on the ball enough. They don't appreciate how important it is for controlling trajectory, distance and direction." Parnevik is what is known as a "shut-face" player, which means he keeps the club slightly closed throughout the backswing, then hits what amounts to a slight intentional pull. David Duval and Lee Trevino are also "shut-face" players. This is most evident in frame 2—the toe of the club is angled slightly away from his body.

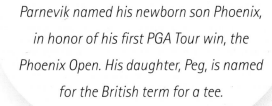

Parnevik named his newborn son Phoenix, in honor of his first PGA Tour win, the Phoenix Open. His daughter, Peg, is named for the British term for a tee.

5

6

7

8

1

2

3

4

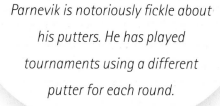

Parnevik is notoriously fickle about his putters. He has played tournaments using a different putter for each round.

PARNEVIK ADJUSTS HIS HANDS ON THE GRIP TO CHANGE THE trajectory and length of his shots. Here, he's choking down slightly—several inches of the grip are exposed at the top—to hit a shorter, more controlled shot. In frame 4, Parnevik's clubface is slightly more shut—pointing at the sky—than the angle of his left arm, the same as it was halfway back in frame 2 of the face-on view. The most notable feature of his swing, and the reason why Parnevik is so accurate, is shown in frame 6. He retains the triangle created by the chest and arms long after the ball is gone. He has turned his arms and shoulders through the ball as a consistent unit, without any extra moving parts.

5

6

7

8

1

2

3

4

PARNEVIK MAKES AN AGGRESSIVE, DOWNWARD STRIKE AT THE ball, so he kicks his right knee in slightly at address (frame 1), to help promote this move. He takes the club back perfectly on plane, with the face "looking" at the ball slightly—which means he's keeping the face pointed more toward the ground. Because of the downward blow, Parnevik's finish position is shorter than that of many other players. With this 6-iron, his hands barely finish above his head.

Parnevik is one of the most prolific birdie-makers on the US Tour, finishing in the top ten in that category for three consecutive years.

5

6

7

8

PRIVATE JETS AND FIRST-CLASS TRAVEL ARE A WAY OF LIFE FOR *professional golfers of today. Tiger Woods plays in a European Tour event in Dubai, catches his private jet Sunday night and is back home by Monday and ready to play in Florida. Gary Player played the international schedule that is so common today, but he did it 30 years before anyone else, and started at time when airplane trips between his native South Africa and America took days, not hours.*

Gary Player

Player started out as an assistant teaching pro at age 18, honing his game to make a run for the South African tour. He won enough to inspire confidence in some members at the club where he worked, and they sponsored a run through some other events around Africa. Player won the Egyptian Open, and the check there was enough to get him to England to play some events on the European Tour. He never looked back. By the end of 1959, Player had won his first major, the British Open (at Muirfield), along with the South African Open, Australian PGA Championship and Kentucky Derby Open on the American tour. He set up a schedule he would keep until he relocated to the United States in the late 1970s. He routinely played events on five continents in a given season—North and South America, Africa, Europe and Australia—and sometimes added a sixth when he

played the odd Asian tour event. Combine the travel wear he endured for three decades with the fact that, at 5-foot-7, Player was always struggling to get more distance, and his accomplishments are even more impressive. In addition to three British Opens, Player won the 1962 and 1972 PGA Championships (the second under full-time armed guard because of death threats over his native South Africa's racial policies), the 1965 US Open and the 1961, 1974 and 1978 Masters tournaments. The '78 Masters win came when Player was 42 years old. But he had the body of someone 15 years younger because of an exhaustive exercise routine he has kept up even to this day to fight off the ill effects of all the travel. Player is still competitive into his late 60s on the Senior Tour. If he didn't reach his goal of being the best of all time, it certainly wasn't for lack of effort.

1

2

3

4

Player has won more than 160 tournaments in his career-on six continents and in five decades. In 1972, he won tournaments in the United States, England, Spain, Brazil, Australia and South Africa.

PLAYER HAS BEEN ABLE TO GET MORE OUT OF HIS SMALL FRAME

than any other golfer in history—both in yardage and durability. He had to work constantly just to be able to drive the ball near the tour average in length. His preferred way to do it was to hit a controlled hook, which rolls longer than a fade. He's also kept himself in incredible condition—he's still competitive on the Senior Tour in his mid-60s because he has got the body of a 45 year-old. These pictures were taken when Player was 60, and he was still very flexible. Frames 2 and 3 show just how well Player still gets extension away from the ball, and the amount of turn he is able to produce. In frame 5, Player drives his legs and hips aggressively toward the target, another source of power. "Gary swings using the big muscles and not by relying on the inconsistent hands and arms," said *Golf Digest* teaching professional, Tim Mahoney.

5

6

7

8

In his 2001 Senior PGA Tour season, Player weighed 145 pounds, five pounds less than his playing weight in 1960.

PLAYER SETS UP WITH HIS HIPS SLIGHTLY open to the target line to accommodate his signature swing trigger. He kicks his left knee back, away from the target to initiate his backswing. That kicked knee and his left heel coming off the ground in frame 4 help Player get the maximum amount of turn. At the top of the back-swing, he has the club in a 25-year-old's position—perfectly parallel to the ground and pointing right at the camera with a square face.

1

2

3

4

5

6

7

8

1

2

3

4

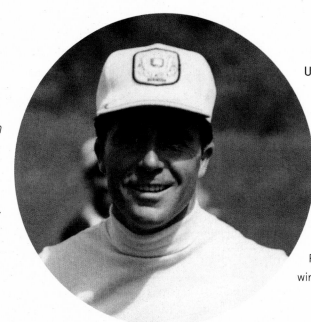

Player is one of only five players to win the career grand slam. Tiger Woods, Jack Nicklaus, Ben Hogan and Gene Sarazen are the others.

UNLIKE CONTEMPORARIES JACK NICKLAUS, ARNOLD Palmer and Lee Trevino, Player has never had a major back injury and hasn't had to alter his swing much as a concession to age. Part of that has to do with Player's fanatical zeal in exercising, which he has been doing since long before it became popular. But it also has to do with how efficient Player's motion is, and the relatively small amount of strain it puts on his back. He uses all of the big muscles in his back and legs together—this is clear in frame 6, at impact—so none bear too much of a burden. Player has talked openly about wanting to be the first man to win in six decades, the 1950s, '60s, '70s, '80s, '90s and 2000s.

5

6

7

8

WITH THE GAME BEING DOMINATED BY ACCOMPLISHED YOUNG PLAYERS
*like Tiger Woods, David Duval, Phil Mickelson and Ernie Els, it's easy to forget
that the last generation of champions—players like Nick Price, Curtis Strange
and Tom Kite-matured a little later as players. Price is the perfect example. He
built a nice record playing in Africa and Europe through the early 1980s, but
didn't explode into prominence until his mid-30s.*

Nick Price

In a 28-month stretch, Price won 17 tournaments worldwide, including three majors, and was in contention nearly every time he teed it up. As hot as Woods was through 2000, players active during both streaks are hard-pressed to pick which stretch was more dominating.

Price turned pro at age 20, in 1977, and worked his way onto the South African tour. He won his first tournament in 1979, the Asseng Invitational in South Africa, then made a quantum leap when he won the 1980 Canon European Masters.

Price stayed in Europe until 1983, when he won the World Series of Golf—a victory that made him exempt on the American tour. He then spent the next six years refining his swing in relative obscurity, finishing between 22nd and 80th on the money list each year, but never winning. Years of work with *Golf Digest* teaching professional, David Leadbetter, started to pay

dividends in 1991, when Price won the Byron Nelson and Canadian Open and jumped to 7th on the money list. That was just the start of what would be a torrid streak of golf. In 1992, Price won his first major, the PGA Championship at Bellerive. The win seemed to trigger something in him, because he immediately set off on that other-worldy stretch.

He won four times in 1993, including the Players Championship, and won the money title. In 1994, he won six times, including the British Open and PGA back to back, and a then-record $1.49 million. Price even won his two majors that year in Woodsian style—going birdie-eagle-par to beat Jesper Parnevik in the British and lapping the field by six at the PGA. Price has remained competitive into his mid-40s (even with a balky putter) and still strikes the ball well enough to get back to those glory days-if only for a week here and there.

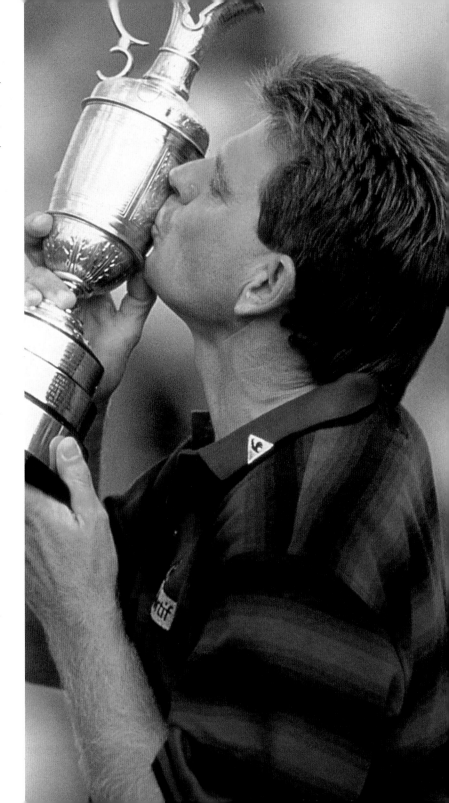

1

2

3

4

PRICE'S SWING IS AS TECHNICALLY SOUND AS ANY. IN FACT,
his peers voted it the best one in professional golf in a 1994 *Golf Digest*
survey. Price just makes his swing at a quicker tempo than most. "It doesn't
matter what swing tempo you have, as long as you're the same speed back
and through," said Johnny Miller. "Nick Price is quick both back and
through. Amateurs get into problems when they go slow-slow-slow-then-
fast." When Price started out as a professional, he had a swing that was
looser, longer and slower—and he was much more inconsistent. He
tightened—and quickened—up, and the results have been nothing but
positive. He starts from a sturdy base, with his legs slightly bowlegged,
which makes it easier to create resistance between his hips and upper body.
Price makes a full turn and gets his left shoulder completely under his chin,
then makes a slight hip slide toward the target (in frame 5), his left knee
has moved outside his foot.

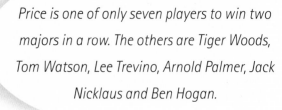

*Price is one of only seven players to win two
majors in a row. The others are Tiger Woods,
Tom Watson, Lee Trevino, Arnold Palmer, Jack
Nicklaus and Ben Hogan.*

5

6

7

8

1

2

3

4

PRICE ADDRESSES THE BALL WITH EVERYTHING—SHOULDERS, HIPS
and feet—square to the target, and plays the ball nearer the toe of the club, because he's going to swing through from inside the line. Like all great ball strikers, Price reduces the things that can go wrong in the swing by keeping his spine angle constant throughout, which prevents him from having to make adjustments with his arms or hands. Many amateur players lose their posture and move into a more upright position at the top of the backswing. Then, they have to get back into address posture to be able to hit the ball solidly.

"I've always been a fan of his action. It's so simple, and when he's swinging well, it's very, very good. But then, it has to be. Nick's tempo is faster than most people's, so he has less time to make any in-swing adjustments."

Golf Digest *teaching professional* **Peter Kostis.**

5

6

7

8

1

2

3

4

PRICE HITS LOW, STRAIGHT SHOTS BECAUSE HE "COVERS" THE ball so well—at impact, his left wrist is flat and his right wrist is bent toward the target, which reduces the effective loft on the club and helps promote solid, flush contact. He's transferring all of his energy into a direct hit on the ball. Price's only break in form is most visible from this angle. In frame 2, he has the club a little bit too upright. It should be pointing down directly at the ball. But by frame 3, he has made a little loop at the top that compensates, and now the club is back perfectly on line.

*Price grew up in Rhodesia (now Zimbabwe),
where all young men had to serve in the military.
Price was an air force fighter pilot who flew
combat missions over Africa.*

5

6

7

8

IF JACK NICKLAUS' LEGACY IS HIS AWESOME TOURNAMENT RECORD *and Arnold Palmer's is the blossoming of golf on television, then Chi Chi Rodriguez's legacy is his touch with the average fan. Rodriguez was a respectable player on the PGA Tour for 20 years and had even more success as a senior, winning nearly 30 events, but he will always be remembered as both a showman and an ambassador.*

Chi Chi Rodriguez

His sword-fighting routine after a made putt is one of the most famous in all of sports, and he still attracts some of the biggest galleries in the senior game, rivaled only by those following Nicklaus and Palmer. Rodriguez has come a long way from the streets of Rio Pedras, Puerto Rico.

That Juan Rodriguez even made it to the professional tour was an upset. He never had any real equipment as a kid—just a branch from a tree to swing and a balled-up tin can to whack. He worked as a caddie until he turned 19, then joined the army. After his hitch, he turned pro and started playing the PGA Tour in 1960. It took him three years to win his first event, the 1963 Denver Open, and he won only eight events in 21 seasons. But Rodriguez was always a crowd—and sponsor—favorite. In an era when even the best players had to grind week to week to

earn a decent living, Rodriguez actually enjoyed bantering with fans and socializing with sponsors. He knew golf was entertainment, and he intended to give every fan in his gallery his or her money's worth for the entire 18 holes. That he could work in some occasional tournament success in the process was a bonus.

Rodriguez has tirelessly promoted the game in both the United States and in Puerto Rico and has raised millions of dollars for his foundation, which helps disadvantaged children. Without the efforts of Rodriguez, Palmer and few other legends from the 1960s and 1970s who were willing to endlessly gladhand and schmooze sponsors, the Senior Tour wouldn't have been nearly as successful as it has been. Some things are more important than tournament wins. Rodriguez knows that better than any other player.

1   2   3   4

"People don't know it, but if Chi Chi Rodriguez putted like Nicklaus and Palmer, there wouldn't have been a Nicklaus or Palmer." Johnny Miller.

RODRIGUEZ'S SWING HAS ONE THING IN COMMON WITH THE swings of the other self-taught players in this book. It doesn't look like anybody else's in the book. Rodriguez learned to play by experimenting, and his swing, like Lee Trevino's, is a collection of improvisations perfected over the years. Rodriguez lashes at the ball to get the most power he can from his small size, but when his swing is captured by the camera, his position at the most important point—impact—is perfect. Rodriguez squats a little bit at impact and has an idiosyncratic head turn just before, but, in total, the improvised parts work very well together. In his prime, he could hit the ball longer, pound for pound, than anyone else on tour.

5   6   7   8

1   2   3   4

Rodriguez has won two senior majors, the 1986 Senior Players Championship and the 1987 PGA Seniors' Championship. Jack Nicklaus beat him in an 18-hole play-off at the 1991 US Senior Open.

AT ADDRESS, RODRIGUEZ STANDS FAR AWAY FROM the ball, which gives him a flat, wide swing path. His has a little loop at the top of his backswing, and brings the club back down to the ball on a slightly steeper plane. Rodriguez relies quite a bit on timing and feel through impact, turning the club over with his hands and forearms to hit a distance-producing draw. This forearm rotation creates the low, post-impact position shown in frame 7. Rodriguez wraps the club around his back at the finish and gets into a classic, high left-side position. In this position, he actually looks like a lot of modern players.

5   6   7   8

WHEN A PROFESSIONAL GOLFER TELLS THE STORY OF WORKING HIS WAY *up through the game's minor leagues, he's usually talking about some sunny minitour in Florida. Vijay Singh served his apprenticeship hitting balls by himself at the end of a range hacked out of the rain forest in Borneo. He beat pile after pile of balls because there was nothing else to do, and because, in his mind, it was the surest way to find a swing that would work in tournament golf.*

Vijay Singh

34

Singh made his way around the fringes of the golf world, winning his first tournament in Malaysia in 1984, then heading for Africa in the late 1980s.

By the early 1990s, Singh had qualified for the European Tour, where he won six times from 1990 to 1994.

He then decided to bring his game to the United States and the PGA Tour. He played a partial schedule in 1993, but that quickly changed after he won the Buick Classic. He finished 19th on the money list playing in only 14 events and was named the tour's rookie of the year. Since then, he's been a regular fixture, but nobody ever considered him a special threat in majors because of a serious Achilles'

heel—his putting stroke. Singh has struggled with the yips since early in his career, and has gone from putting cross-handed to using a mid-length putter that anchors in his gut, and back again. But at the 1998 PGA Championship at Sahalee, Singh put together four good putting rounds to beat Steve Stricker. Even more shocking was his performance at the 2000 Masters—where a poor putter is quickly exposed. Singh didn't three-putt one green on his way to a dominating display at Augusta. Singh shot rounds of 70-67 on the weekend to win by three, making him the only player besides Tiger Woods to win two majors since the end of 1998.

1

2

3

4

SINGH'S APPROACH IS UNCOMPLICATED. HE FOCUSES ON fundamentals—set-up, arm swing, body motion and pace—then works at them at the range relentlessly. "Vjiay practices harder than any other tour player, and he can practice longer than anybody else because he's strong and tireless," said Rick Smith, a *Golf Digest* teaching professional. "Every day, he swings a customized lead driver. An ordinary person can barely lift it, but he swings it 100 times a day and can hit the ball 230 yards with it." Singh, a tall player, has an athletic set up. In the backswing, he makes no effort to cock his wrists—they do it on their own from momentum. Combine Singh's strength, flexibility and the late wrist cock he shows in frame 5 and it's no surprise that he's one of the five longest hitters on the PGA Tour.

Singh learned to play from old issues of Golf Digest, *copying Tom Weiskopf's swing from sequence photographs—the same ones shown here on page 169.*

5

6

7

8

1

2

3

4

SINGH'S POSTURE IS COMFORTABLE—HE DOESN'T STAND TOO upright, and has a gentle bend in his knees. He has plenty of room to make a full turn and swing the club from the inside. In frame 4, Singh's club is in a great position—and the clubface angle matches the angle of his left arm perfectly—pointing right at the camera. At impact, you can see the glint of the sun from the clubface. It's exactly square. Singh grips the club so lightly, you can see his hands falling off the club a little bit after impact.

In his nomadic travels, Singh has won tournaments in 14 different countries— Malaysia, France, Nigeria, Ivory Coast, Morocco, Zimbabwe, Spain, Germany, England, South Africa, Sweden, Taiwan, the United States and Singapore.

5

6

7

8

1

2

3

4

5

6

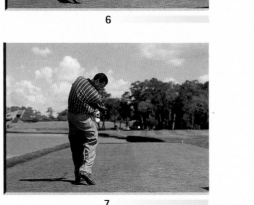

7

8

SINGH MAKES A CLASSIC, SAM SNEAD KIND OF MOVE IN frame 2. He kicks his right knee in as he starts his backswing. It's a trigger for the beginning of his hip turn. "At the top, Vijay's shoulders turn more than 90 degrees, his hips just over 45 degrees—one of the fullest turns on tour," Smith said. In that top-of-the-backswing position, Singh's arms create a perfect triangle, and his spine angle is the same as it was at address, one of the reasons Singh is such a good long-iron player. Singh uses the heavy club to work the muscles in his arms, chest and back, but it also forces him to keep a rhythmic tempo and make a nice, slow transition at the top of the backswing.

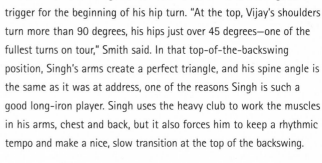

As a PGA Tour rookie in 1993, Singh shot a second-round 63 at the PGA Championship, tying the record for the low round in major championship history. He shot 73-70 on the weekend to finish tied for fourth.

SAM SNEAD HAD PHENOMENAL SUCCESS—MORE PGA TOUR
*wins than anyone else—and he lasted as a competitive force well into
his 50s. But the hallmark of his career is something that he didn't do.
Despite all of those wins, including seven major championships,
Snead never won a US Open. In fact, his near misses have become
epic tales.*

Sam Snead

At the 1939 Open, Snead thought he needed to make a four to win. This was before scoreboards were an integral part of the tournament golf landscape and, actually, all he needed to do was to make a bogey six to get into a play-off. Playing aggressively, he made a triple bogey and lost.

If anything, Snead suffered from comparisons with his contemporaries. Snead, Byron Nelson and Ben Hogan were born less than a year apart and came into the game in the same period—as a result, their games and records were inexorably linked. Nelson had an incendiary run of golf, then retired young. Hogan rebuilt his game, nearly died in a car accident, then triumphantly returned.

Comparitively speaking, Snead's story didn't have as much drama. All he did was last and last. When Snead joined the professional tour full-time in 1937, he made an immediate impact. He won his first event in Oakland, and promoters played up the fact that Snead was a country boy from West Virginia. Golf had a new folk hero. Snead won five tournaments (and finished second in his first US Open) in 1937, then won eight more events in 1938.

Losses to Paul Runyan in the final of the 1938 PGA Championship and Ralph Guldahl in the 1938 Masters reinforced Snead's reputation as someone who folded under pressure. It wasn't until the 1942 PGA, which Snead won just before entering the Navy in World War II, that he could start shedding that label. Snead would go on to win six more majors, the 1949 and 1951 PGA, the Masters in 1949, 1952 and 1954 and the 1946 British Open. But he has proven to be the game's most durable player, winning into his 50s on the regular tour and adding six PGA Seniors titles.

1

2

3

4

Snead won his first PGA Tour event in 1936, the West Virginia Closed Pro, and his last in 1965 at the Greensboro Open—a span of 29 years. When he won in Greensboro, he was the oldest player to ever win a PGA Tour event.

IF BEN HOGAN WENT ON A QUEST TO DISCOVER THE PERFECT mechanics of the golf swing, Snead was the polar opposite. Snead was the original "feel" player. His graceful, athletic swing was both natural and uncomplicated. "I didn't see any sense in making the game any harder than it is," Snead said. "When I got my first set of steel shafts, I'd hit one 5-iron 160 yards and the next maybe 210. That's when I started practicing rhythm. I've never worked on anything else since." Of all the players from the 1930s and 1940s—including Byron Nelson—Snead has the swing that most resembles the one many tour players use today. Compare frame 3 here to a similar position in, for example, Vijay Singh's swing and you'll notice a striking similarity. Snead's position in frame 6 is classic as well. He's created a lot of lag, and has retained the distance between his knees—a slight "squat" position—which gave him incredible consistency. Snead's swing also aged better than any in the game. He was competitive on the regular tour long into his 50s and could still hit 250-yard drives well into his 70s.

5

6

7

8

GOLF IS A GRIND—NOT AN EXPLOSION, LIKE FOOTBALL.
Championship golfers often fade away from competition, delighting their fans more just by showing up at a Senior Tour event. The game wasn't ready to lose Payne Stewart in the way it did. A malfunction in his leased jet depressurized the cabin and killed all aboard before the jet crashed to earth on October 25, 1999.

Payne Stewart

Stewart had just finished one of his most triumphant seasons, winning the US Open and AT&T Pebble Beach National Pro-am and anchoring the victorious 1999 Ryder Cup team. He had come all the way back from a slump that stemmed from an ill-advised equipment change and had become a happier, more approachable friend and fellow competitor.

Stewart, like so many of the other players in this book, got into the game because of his father, who played in the 1955 US Open at Olympic. Stewart graduated from Southern Methodist University in 1979 and made it onto the tour for good in 1981 after a successful stint in Asia, where he won the Indonesian and Asian Opens.

Stewart won his first PGA Tour event the next year at the Quad Cities Open and improved his standing on the money list in four out of the next five years. In 1989, he won his first major championship, the PGA at Kemper, by shooting a final-round 67 to come from six strokes back and win by a shot. Stewart suffered a neck injury that kept him out of the game for almost three months in early 1991, but he had recovered enough by mid-summer to win his second major, the US Open at Hazeltine. He beat Scott Simpson in an 18-hole play-off for his only win of the season.

By 1994, Stewart had switched equipment and started to struggle with his swing. He bottomed out at 123rd on the money list, but recovered in 1995 to win the Shell Houston Open. In 1999, he had just started to play as well as he had in the early 1990s, winning the AT&T Pebble Beach National Pro-Am and beating Phil Mickelson head to head at Pinehurst to win his second US Open title. Then came the plane crash that stunned the golf world. Stewart was 42 years old.

1

2

3

4

"Payne was a devout patriot. This was never more obvious than when he talked about the importance of the Ryder Cup and American pride. The Open was the championship of America!"

Golf Digest *teaching professional,* **Chuck Cook.**

THESE PHOTOS, TAKEN JUST DAYS BEFORE STEWART WAS KILLED, show why he had such an enduring career. His flowing swing was smooth and rhythmic—and picture perfect in every position. Stewart was an excellent ball-striker, delivering the club precisely time after time. The finish is classic—high hands, weight on the outside of his left foot. Like many other good ball-strikers, Stewart takes the club back with a slightly closed face—shown in frame 2. But the way he moves his lower body in the swing shows why that closed clubface didn't produce a hook. In frames 2 and 3, Stewart turns his hips to start the backswing, but on the way down, he slides them toward the target first, then turns them after impact. If he didn't get his hips a little bit ahead of the ball at impact, he'd hit a low hook. As a result, Stewart's hips stay square to the ball for a long time through the swing—through frames 5, 6 and 7. Players who try to hit a fade have turned their hips through much more to the left by impact. Stewart's swing is also a model for keeping the head steady throughout. It stays in the same position in frames 1 through 7, with the shoulders and hips coiling and uncoiling underneath. It's no great surprise that Stewart was exceptionally accurate.

5

6

7

8

FROM THIS ANGLE, STEWART'S SWING LOOKS

very much like that of Bobby Jones (see pages 66-67). The only difference is that Jones didn't hold his wrist cock as long into the downswing—a concession to the much more flexible hickory shafts of the day. Stewart's takeaway, shown in frame 2, is highlighted by his extended arm position. The club is nearly at waist height, yet he has not cocked his wrists at all. This extension increases the length of the swing, which gives him more time to generate speed on the way down. By frame 3, Stewart has only just started to cock his wrists, but he has cocked them before he reaches the top of the backswing in frame 4. It is important to have control of the clubhead at this point, without any loose movement. Otherwise, crisp ballstriking is impossible.

1

2

3

4

5

6

7

8

1

2

3

4

"His feel and great hands gave him an advantage. If he got into a tough up-and-down situation, Payne relished the challenge, where others might have felt daunted by the difficulty."

Golf Digest *teaching professional,* **Chuck Cook**.

GOLF DIGEST TEACHING PROFESSIONAL CHUCK

Cook, Stewart's long-time teacher, felt that Stewart's swing was comparable to the "classic" swings of other generations. "Payne's footwork is a lot like Sam Snead's, Tom Weiskopf's, or any other player who has a lot of lag in his golf swing. He swings fairly flat-footed, rolling off the inside of his left foot on the backswing—hardly lifting his left heel—and then rolling off his right foot on the downswing." By the time Stewart's swing reaches frame 5, his right heel is still close to the ground. He's had to time his lower body turn to let the club catch up. Other players have already moved completely to the left side by this time.

5

6

7

8

HAL SUTTON'S STORY IS A TALE OF TWO CAREERS. HE WAS 11TH *on the money list as a rookie, way back in 1982, then won the Players Championship and PGA Championship as a second-year pro—beating Jack Nicklaus by a shot at the PGA. Sutton led the PGA Tour in earnings and was on top of the world. The good times continued through 1986, when Sutton won both the Phoenix Open and Memorial tournaments.*

Hal Sutton

But then Sutton started experimenting with his swing, trying to hit the ball higher and longer. By 1992, he had cratered, earning only $39,294 in 29 tournaments and losing his card. After another horrific season in 1993 ($74,144 in 29 events) Sutton was forced to take a one-time special exemption available to players in the top 50 in career earnings to avoid having to go through Q-school again.

He got back together with his college coach, Floyd Horgen, and erased all of the swing changes he had undertaken and got back to basics—the shorter, big-muscle action that produced incredible accuracy and reliability.

Sutton took advantage of his last chance, rebounding to 29th in earnings on the strength of four top-10 finishes. That was just the start of the second-coming of Hal Sutton.

By 1998, Sutton had found the combination that had worked so well in the early 1980s—fairways (top five in total driving) and greens (top seven in greens in regulation). He even improved his putting. At the season-ending Tour Championship at East Lake Country Club, Sutton birdied the first play-off hole to beat Vijay Singh. He jumped to fifth on the money list in the process. And while beating Nicklaus at the PGA was his biggest moment in the first part of his career, anchoring the the 1999 American Ryder Cup team and facing down Tiger Woods at the 2000 Players Championship (Sutton won by a shot) have to be the highlights of his second phase. Now in his mid-40s, Sutton shows no signs of losing his competitiveness on the regular tour, and should be dangerous as a senior.

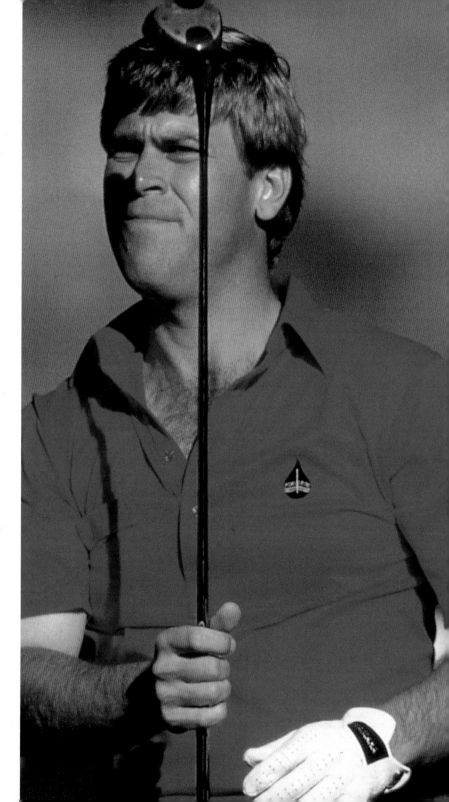

1

2

3

4

AFTER STRUGGLING FOR MOST OF THE 1990s, SUTTON GOT BACK to his original game—letting the big muscles drive a swing built for accuracy over power. Sutton's goal is to maintain the triangle between his arms and shoulders for as long as possible during the backswing, while keeping his lower body as quiet as possible. He sets up with his weight already shifted slightly to the right to kick-start his backswing. In frame 4, Sutton has made a big shift to the right while moving his lower body very little. Strangely enough, Sutton has has always been compared to Jack Nicklaus—both are big, blond and stocky—but the similarities end there. Nicklaus's head stays stable throughout his swing and he pivots around a fixed point. Sutton hits with a moving pivot—he shifts well behind the ball in the backswing.

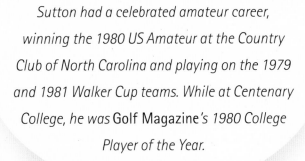

Sutton had a celebrated amateur career, winning the 1980 US Amateur at the Country Club of North Carolina and playing on the 1979 and 1981 Walker Cup teams. While at Centenary College, he was **Golf Magazine**'s *1980 College Player of the Year.*

5

6

7

8

Need proof that Augusta National favors players who hit a high fade? Hal Sutton, a low, straight hitter, has made the cut in only three of 13 appearances at The Masters.

ONE OF THE MAJOR BENEFITS OF SUTTON'S SWING IS THAT it doesn't cause a lot of stress on his back or hips, plus it doesn't require a lot of flexibility. In frame 4, at the top of Sutton's backswing, he never gets to parallel, and he doesn't have a radical shoulder turn like an Ernie Els or Fred Couples. Those are two good reasons he could stay competitive until he gets to the Senior Tour—assuming he continues to putt well. Compare the position of Sutton's shoulders in frame 1 and frame 6. They are identical—a hallmark of accurate drivers. Sutton isn't afraid to hit a driver even on the tightest holes—like the 18th at the TPC at Sawgrass, where water guards the entire left side. Sutton split the fairway when he beat Woods at the 2000 Players Championship.

1

2

3

4

5

6

7

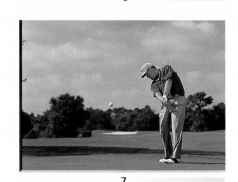

8

1

2

In 1999 and 2000, Hal Sutton had a combined 24 top-ten finishes, more than any player except Tiger Woods.

5

6

3

7

4

8

IN FRAME 2, YOU CAN SEE JUST HOW WELL SUTTON RETAINS
the triangle he created at address. He still has it in frame 3, then lets his
right elbow cock in frame 4. In frame 5, Sutton's club is in perfect
position—it bisects the space between his two forearms. At impact the only
difference between this and the address position is the hip turn and
kicked-in right knee. After impact, Sutton lets the club chase down the
target line well after the ball has left. His finish is upright and balanced.
Even with a 6-foot-1, 210-pound frame, Sutton isn't a long hitter. But from
1998 through 2000, he was in the top 30 in driving accuracy each year.

LEE TREVINO HAS ONE OF THOSE STORIES YOU'D SWEAR WAS MADE UP *for a movie of the week. He turned pro right after a four-year hitch in the Marines and perfected his swing playing in money matches with locals who frequented the El Paso course at which he was an assistant pro. Not only did he build a swing that would keep the ball low under the wind, but he became a pure ball-striker, someone who could manufacture any kind of shot to hit it close.*

Lee Trevino

He even made money swinging things other than golf clubs. One of his favorite hustles was to bet some vulnerable pigeon that he could beat him over nine holes using only a pop bottle covered with electrical tape. Trevino would then bat the golf ball around with the bottle and use his putter on the greens. He usually broke par that way. So when Trevino made it into the field of the 1967 US Open at Baltusrol, hitting shots with real-life clubs wasn't as much of a challenge. A virtual unknown, Trevino finished fifth and emerged as one of the game's most charismatic stars, charming galleries with his almost non-stop banter and pointed wit.

In 1968, Trevino won his first major, the US Open, and did it in style. He was the first to shoot four rounds in the 60s in the national championship. Pressed for an encore, he came up with something suitable.

Trevino went head to head with Jack Nicklaus when Nicklaus was at the height of his powers and came away victorious. Not only did Trevino beat Nicklaus in an 18-hole play-off to win the 1972 US Open, he got Jack again in Britain later that summer, chipping in down the stretch to win his second consecutive British Open title. Combine those successes with Trevino's 1974 and 1984 PGA Championship wins (the '84 title came when he was 44 years old) and it's easy to see why he ranks as one of a handful of the greatest players in the history of the game. Trevino did nothing to tarnish that legacy with his work on the Senior Tour. One of the two winningest Seniors in the history of that tour, Trevino has added four Senior majors to his resume, including the 1990 Senior Open. He also stayed competitive into his 60s, something few seniors can claim.

 **1**

 **2**

 **3**

 **4**

Trevino won five Vardon Trophies for low scoring average on the PGA Tour, the most of any tour player.

TREVINO TRULY HAS A HOMEMADE SWING. "GOLF IS A GAME of numbers," he said. "They don't draw pictures by that score you write down." He built it himself to suit the conditions in which he played growing up—dry courses with high winds. Trevino has always favored a low, hard fade, which he hits with a flat, blocking motion. Trevino's excellent hands and touch let him create the shot he needs. Trevino starts out with an extra-strong grip, like a lot of self-taught players. It's the most comfortable way to put the hands on the club. In frame 2, Trevino is taking the club back with a closed face—one reason he hits the ball so low. He makes a short backswing, then slides his hips and left knee through impact. Trevino has never been exceptionally long, but he's known as one of the greatest ball-strikers in the history of golf.

 **5**

 **6**

 **7**

 **8**

TREVINO'S DRAMATICALLY UNORTHODOX SET-UP

is most noticeable from this angle. He sets up with his shoulders slightly open to the target line, but his feet well open. He clearly prefers to play a fade—sliding the club down the target line, then bringing it back across his body after impact. He brings the club back on a relatively steep plane—the butt end points inside the ball in frame 3—then redirects it dramatically flatter in frame 5. It goes even flatter in frame 5, but the butt of the club is pointing right at the ball. Trevino makes more flush contact than almost any other pro on either the senior or regular tour.

Trevino has won more than twice as much money, more than $9 million, in his Senior Tour career than he did on the PGA Tour.

1

2

3

4

5

6

7

8

1

2

3

4

Trevino is the master of the witty aside. Once, when a female fan was gushing over his every swing at the practice range, Trevino turned to her and said, "What did you expect from a million-dollar winner, lady? Ground balls?"

CONTRAST HOW FLAT TREVINO IS AT IMPACT WITH frame 3 in this sequence. Here, he has the club almost vertical to the ground, with the clubface closed. No other pro has ever won anything using this kind of swing—it is truly unique. Because he doesn't turn his hips much, the club immediately flattens out on the first move toward the ball. Trevino's right shoulder works under his left. After impact, he keeps his head low, which is the classic image we have of him. Trevino's finish is low as well. Compare that to the high finish of a high-ball hitter like Jack Nicklaus.

5

6

7

8

ONLY TWO PLAYERS CHALLENGED JACK NICKLAUS' SUPREMACY IN THE
1970s and early 80s. Lee Trevino was Nicklaus' main foil in the early 1970s, while Tom Watson took over from Nicklaus as the world's best player in the late 1970s and early 80s. In his prime, Watson was the best ball-striker in the game— he still hits the ball as well as he ever did on the Senior Tour—and he was automatic on putts under six feet. From 1977 to 1984, Watson had no peer in golf.

Tom Watson

Nobody ever had much doubt that Watson would become a fine professional player after graduating from Stanford in 1971. He had a second-place finish in his first full season on tour, in 1972, then two more in 1973. In 1975, Watson won his first title in grand fashion, beating Tom Weiskopf and J.C. Snead at the Western Open.

Two weeks later, he won the first of his five British Opens, beating Jack Newton by a shot in an 18-hole play-off. He failed to win an event in 1976, but that would be the last time he would go winless until 1985. In 1977, Watson finally eclipsed Nicklaus, winning the Masters, then shooting a final round 65 to Nicklaus' 66 in the British Open at Turnberry.

Watson followed his four wins in 1977 with five in 1978, five in 1979, six in 1980 (including the British Open), three in 1981 (including his second Masters) and three more in 1982. One of Watson's wins in 1982 was an instant classic. Stuck in an impossible lie, he chipped in for birdie on the 17th hole at Pebble Beach to beat Nicklaus at the US Open. Watson won the British again in 1983, this time beating Andy Bean and Hale Irwin by a shot. In the seven-year stretch between 1977 and 1984, Watson won seven major championships, 29 PGA Tour events, three Vardon Trophies for low scoring average and was PGA Player of the Year six times. The yips took Watson's putting stoke soon after that, and he won only three tournaments from 1985 to 1998. In 1998, Watson won the Colonial at age 48, and then made a smooth transition to the Senior Tour, where he has been a consistent force ever since. But he'll always be remembered for that brilliant stretch of golf in the late 1970s and early 1980s. Only a few players have ever had such a run.

1

2

3

4

TOM WATSON STRUGGLED EARLY IN HIS CAREER

with spraying the ball off the tee. The crucial change he made is evident here, in a sequence taken in his prime, the late 1970s. Before, Watson's right leg was too loose during the backswing, which didn't allow him to build full resistance for his upper body coil. It also cost him consistency. Watson firmed up his right leg and slightly shortened his swing and immediately improved his ball-striking. He went on to win eight majors between 1975 and 1983. Even with the somewhat shortened swing, Watson still gets the club past parallel in frame 5. In frame 8, long after impact, Watson's arms are still fully extended and traveling down the target line. It isn't surprising that he was—and still is—one of the premier ball-strikers of all time.

From 1974 to 1984, Watson finished in the top ten in eight of the ten US Opens in which he played.

5

6

7

8

1

2

3

4

THIS SEQUENCE, TAKEN SHORTLY BEFORE WATSON

joined the Senior Tour and more than 20 years after the one shown on the previous page, shows just how well his swing has aged. Watson's action hasn't changed much over time. Like Nicklaus, Watson has a one-piece takeaway, and doesn't cock his wrists until late in the backswing. If anything, Watson gets a little more turn here, in his 40s, (frame 4) than he did in the previous sequence. Even the impact position is similar. The one concession Watson has made to "modern" times is his finish. He now ends in much more upright position, as opposed to his old "reverse C" finish. It's easier on his back.

5

6

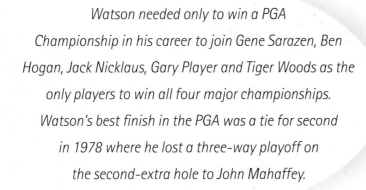

Watson needed only to win a PGA Championship in his career to join Gene Sarazen, Ben Hogan, Jack Nicklaus, Gary Player and Tiger Woods as the only players to win all four major championships. Watson's best finish in the PGA was a tie for second in 1978 where he lost a three-way playoff on the second-extra hole to John Mahaffey.

7

8

KARRIE WEBB HAS BEEN DOMINATING THE LPGA LIKE TIGER WOODS HAS *the PGA Tour, but her route into professional golf couldn't have been more different. Webb grew up in a remote part of Queensland, Australia, and didn't start playing golf until age eight. She didn't draw much interest from American college golf programs and didn't really blossom as a player until age 20, when she won the 1994 Australian Stroke Play championship.*

Karrie Webb

But in the short span since, she has won more than 25 events worldwide and climbed to the top position in the women's game. Like Woods, she combines length, precise iron play and clutch putting into a formidable package—and she hasn't shown any signs of letting up.

Almost nobody paid any attention when Webb, an excruciatingly shy woman from the tiny Australian town of Ayr, turned pro in 1994. She played events on the women's tour in Europe and the minor-league Futures Tour in the United States and won once. The first blip on the radar screen came in 1995, when she won the Women's British Open (now an LPGA major, but then a WPGET European event) and was the European tour's rookie of the year.

She came to Florida to try for her LPGA card, but took a nasty fall just before the tournament and broke a bone in her wrist. Doctors advised her to put the clubs away until the bone

healed, but she taped it and played in the qualifying tournament anyway and finished second. It didn't take long for her to assert herself on her new tour.

In the second event of her rookie LPGA season in 1997, she won the HEALTHSOUTH Inaugural in a playoff. She won three more events that season, including the tour championship, and became the first woman to win more than $1 million in a season. Webb had her best season to date in 2000. With all the hype surrounding Woods' three-major season, Webb had a year that might have been just as good. She won three times before the season's first major was played, then she won that one, the Nabisco Championship, too, by a record ten shots over Dottie Pepper. At the US Women's Open Webb won the championship and earned enough points to qualify for the LPGA's Hall of Fame. And all of this before her 27th birthday.

1

2

3

4

"Karrie is relentlessly competitive, and she knows she has to continually improve if she wants to stay at the top."

Kelvin Haller, *Webb's coach.*

WEBB HAS WORKED WITH ONLY ONE TEACHER, KELVIN HALLER,

since she started playing as a kid. Haller was one of the better players at the little club in their town, and Webb's parents asked him to give Karrie some pointers. The relationship has flourished, and Webb still makes regular pilgrimages home for fine-tuning. "Karrie's swing is uncomplicated and repeatable," Haller said. "She's always had great rhythm." Although they grew up continents apart, Webb and Tiger Woods have developed swings with some interesting similarities. She sets up with her feet slightly wider than her shoulders, to provide stability when she makes her big backswing. Webb has an exceptionally wide takeaway, as shown in frame 2, and she's flexible enough to get her hands quite far above her head and away from her body, like Woods (frame 5). She makes a graceful, quiet transition at the top, then transmits all of her energy into the ball. Nothing is wasted.

5

6

7

8

1

2

3

4

In five years on the LPGA Tour, Webb made enough money to move to No. 3 on the all-time earnings list. In 2000, she missed becoming the first woman to earn $2 million in a season by less than $125,000.

THE MOST RECOGNIZABLE PART OF WEBB'S SWING comes just before the pictures in this sequence start. She has an unusually large waggle, or swing trigger. She sets up to the ball, then makes an abbreviated takeaway—the club moves back just over waist level. She then pauses briefly and makes her real takeaway. The move helps her stay loose and fluid—instead of stiff—at address, and gives her wrists and arms a preview of what to do in the real swing.

5

6

7

8

WEBB'S MOST COMMON FAULT IS A SLIGHT

sway on the backswing. She takes the club back so wide, she occasionally moves her weight outside of her feet. When that happens, she doesn't strike the ball as consistently. These pictures were taken right after a visit with Haller in Australia. She stays nicely over her feet here. In frame 2, she turns her head slightly during the backswing, a signature Jack Nicklaus move, to help her get more shoulder turn. She even has a little bit of Jack's flying elbow in frame 4.

Webb has won at least two tournaments every season she has been on the LPGA Tour, and has never finished lower than fourth on the money list.

1

2

3

4

5

6

7

8

WHILE AMERICA WAS BUSY BUILDING ITS OWN GOLF STARS
throughout the 1990s, Lee Westwood quietly emerged as one of Europe's next great players. Overshadowed by Colin Montgomerie's streak of seven consecutive money titles on the European Tour, Westwood grew into his role, improving every season since 1995. Along with Sergio Garcia, Darren Clarke and Thomas Bjorn, Westwood represents the next generation of European golf.

Lee Westwood

Westwood picked up the game late, relatively speaking, making his first swings at age 13. By age 20, he had turned pro. Three years later, in 1996, he won his first European Tour title, the Volvo Scandinavian Masters. He made his way slowly up the money list, winning four times in 1998 and three in 1999. He also made a successful foray into the United States in 1998, winning the Freeport McMoran Classic the week before the Masters.

But Westwood showed that the best was yet to come with his play in 2000. He won six tournaments (tying Seve Ballesteros and Nick Faldo for the European Tour record for wins in a season), and finished tied for fifth at the US Open and second at the American Express Championship.

The six wins helped push him to the top of the European money list (with a record E3,125,146) for the first time in his career and capped an ascension from 75th in 1995, sixth in 1996, third in 1997 and 1998 and second in 1999. Westwood also moved into the top five in the world rankings for the first time.

With Tiger Woods, David Duval, Sergio Garcia and Phil Mickelson, Westwood joins a select group of established stars yet to turn 30. The only thing missing on his record is a major championship. Montgomerie is still waiting for his first after seven years as the European Tour's standard-bearer. Westwood probably won't have to wait that long.

 1

 2

 3

 4

In 1999, Westwood won three consecutive tournaments he entered, the TNT Dutch Open, Smurfit European Open (where he came from seven strokes back to beat Darren Clarke) and the Canon European Masters.

WESTWOOD'S SWING IS A PERFECT DEMONSTRATION OF HOW

less-than-ideal moves that compensate for each other can produce great results. At address, he looks very standard—neutral grip, arms hanging comfortably in front of him. But after Westwood reaches the top of his backswing, he starts to lower his head on the way down to impact. Check the photographs of the 100 top players in the game, and 99 of them would have a straight left arm at impact. But if Westwood kept his left arm straight with his lower posture, he'd plow the club into the ground behind the ball. So, at impact, Westwood's left arm has a noticeable bend. In all other respects, Westwood is in good position. His head is behind the ball, he's braced against a firm left leg and his right wrist is cupped, with the right palm facing the target. So Westwood's two swing "faults," a dip in his posture and the bent right arm, marry together to make one of the most solid swings in the pro game.

 5

 6

 7

 8

TO GET SOME PERSPECTIVE ABOUT THE SCALE OF TIGER WOODS' *accomplishments in golf before the age of 30, consider this: by the time Woods became the first player to win four consecutive majors, back in 2001, the debate had already started about whether or not he was the greatest player of all time. He was 26 years old.*

Tiger Woods

Woods has once-in-a-generation talent, and his debut on the PGA Tour was the most anticipated since Jack Nicklaus won the US Open as a rookie in 1960. Woods won three consecutive US Juniors, then three straight US Amateurs before turning professional after his sophomore year at Stanford, in 1997. He won the fifth event he entered as a professional, the Las Vegas Invitational, and earned enough money in seven starts to qualify for the Tour Championship. He has been the dominant player on tour since.

Woods certainly has rare physical gifts: he routinely generates 125 miles per hour of clubhead speed and has hit some of the most freakishly awesome shots in Tour history. But his most important asset has been an almost superhuman ability to focus and eliminate distractions. Even with the massive crowds and squadrons of television cameras following his every swing, he has yet to crumble under final round major championship pressure. By 2003, Woods had won 39 tournaments and eight major championships, and had earned over $10 million more in total career earnings than the next closest player, Davis Love III.

When Woods was a child, he had a chart taped to the back of his bedroom door. It listed all of Nicklaus' scoring and tournament accomplishments, and the age at which Jack completed them. Woods might not have the chart up on the door of his Orlando mansion today, but he's still keenly aware of the accomplishments on that list. Nicklaus' 20 major championships remain Woods' ultimate goal. "I would be very surprised if he doesn't break all of my records," says Nicklaus. "At the rate he's going, it's not such an awfully long haul."

1

2

3

4

5

6

7

8

WOODS HAD ALREADY WON A MAJOR CHAMPIONSHIP AND A
money title—as a second-year player in 1997—when he decided to tear up his swing and start over. His old swing was longer and looser, and Woods didn't want to risk a breakdown under intense tournament pressure. After a year of punishing work with teacher Butch Harmon, Woods' swing morphed into the one you see here—tight, powerful and fully controlled. Woods' arms no longer got trapped behind his body, and his distance control dramatically improved. The positions you see here in frames 5, 6 and 8 are the blueprints for the swing of the future—wide, powerful and graceful, and with incredible balance. The only drawback to this type of action is the stress it puts on the left knee. In frame 7, you can see how much torque is put on the joint. Woods has already had one knee surgery to fix cartilage damage, and he'll probably need another before he quits.

Woods led the PGA Tour in victories—and won Player of the Year honors—in six of his first seven seasons.

1

2

3

4

ONE OF THE MAJOR DIFFERENCES BETWEEN THIS SWING AND ones of players from the 1960s and 1970s is the extension and separation Woods gets away from his body on the downswing. Players like Nicklaus and Johnny Miller had their right arms very close to the body on the bottom of the downswing. Woods' arms have more room to swing freely in front of him. Part of that is from necessity—Woods generates so much speed that he'd hurt himself if he didn't have that much room to swing through. Woods also creates that room by turning so aggressively away from the ball. He's flexible enough to get incredible differentiation between his hip and shoulder turn. The club is in perfect position in frame 4, at the top of the backswing, and all Woods has to do is let the coil unravel. The result? Three hundred yards of carry, or a 245-yard five-iron over water to seal a tournament.

Woods holds the 72-hole scoring record for all four of the major championships.

5

6

7

8

1

2

3

4

*Through his first 28 major championships
as a professional, Woods won eight, finished
in the top 10 in 17—and didn't miss a cut.*

5

6

7

8

IN FRAMES 2 AND 4, YOU CAN SEE HOW SQUARE

Woods' clubface is during the swing. Before he started working with Harmon, Woods had a more closed clubface during his swing, which forced him to really work his lower body to get square. Timing is still an important part of a good swing, but the square face reduces most of the wild hooks and blocks that used to pop up when Woods hit his driver. As Woods has learned to control his power, he has recognized that it isn't necessary to take a big swing at the ball every time. Woods' driving distance average has remained virtually unchanged through his professional career—in an era when most players have gained 15 to 20 yards—but he is still regularly among the tour leaders in greens in regulation. He hit more than 75 per cent in his historic 2000 season—the best percentage of all time.

Frame 1

Frame 2

Colin Montgomerie and Jesper Parnevik

COLIN MONTGOMERIE AND JESPER PARNEVIK HAVE WON a lot of money and Ryder Cup points with vastly different swings. Montgomerie is cut from the same cloth as Nick Faldo— a player whose stock in trade is hitting lots of fairways and keeping the ball in good position. Parnevik has a quick tempo and aggressive move through the ball. He reduces the effective loft on his irons and really compresses the ball at impact, hitting low, long shots. He hits his irons as long—and ocassionally as inaccurately—as anyone in the professional game.

The first frames shown here demonstrate why Parnevik is so much longer than Montgomerie, while the second set show why Monty is more accurate. Montgomerie makes a full backswing and gets significant shoulder turn, but that turn is offset by the big hip turn he also makes. Power comes from the differential between the shoulder turn and the hip turn, as Parnevik demonstrates. Parnevik has less shoulder turn, but he coils very well against his hips. He's storing power, while Montgomerie is leaking it.

In the second photographs, Parnevik has already hit the ball and is beginning his through swing. On most of his shots, he hits an "intentional pull," aiming slightly to the right and pulling across and hitting his shots left, to the target. You can see here that he's collapsed his right leg against his left and fired his hips significantly. Montgomerie keeps nice separation between his legs past impact and lets the club travel on its normal path– slightly outside to in for a gentle fade–through to the finish. Montgomerie doesn't get the most power out of his swing, but he's been very accurate, especially off the tee, throughout his career. It's been putting that has most often let both Parnevik and Montgomerie down in the most important tournaments, although both have been terrific for Europe in the Ryder Cup.

Byron Nelson and Johnny Miller

BYRON NELSON WAS NOT ONLY IN THE RIGHT PLACE at the right time, but he had the skill to take advantage of the innovations in golf equipment. The result was the birth of the "modern" golf swing. Nelson set up to the ball in a much more upright position, and he could keep his wrists cocked in the downswing with his steel-shafted clubs much longer than players using more flexible, hickory-shafted clubs could. His finish position looks much like that of great players today—upright, with the weight balanced over the left leg.

Johnny Miller was always considered a classic swinger of the golf club. His address position is very similar to Nelson's, down to the position of the head (behind the ball) and grip (neutral). Nelson dragged the club away from the ball in the backswing while Miller cocked his wrists early, but toward the top of their backwsing, their positions are virtually identical.

Starting with address, Nelson was more upright all the way through his swing than nearly any other player had been before. That steeper swing plane is one of the reasons he was such a good iron player. With a steep plane, the club comes through the ball in a dramatic downward strike, the perfect way to hit flush, straight shots. Miller at impact had his head much more behind the ball, the start of the "reverse C" position through to the finish. The "reverse C"—where the head and shoulders are tilted back away from the target, so that the back curves into a "C"—was popularized by Jack Nicklaus, who got into the position because of his great leg drive and hip rotation. The generation of players just after Nicklaus—Miller, Tom Weiskopf and Tom Watson are the best examples—were all taught by teachers who were influenced by the success Nicklaus was having on the professional tour.

Frame 1

Frame 2

Frame 1

Frame 2

Jack Nicklaus and Karrie Webb

IT SHOULD COME AS NO SURPRISE THAT PIECES OF Karrie Webb's swing are reminiscent of Jack Nicklaus'. When she was growing up in Ayr, Australia, her teacher, Kelvin Haller, used pictures of Nicklaus as teaching aids. The same factors that helped Nicklaus hit high, powerful, long iron shots—a wide takeway and a big swing arc—help Webb do the same thing on the LPGA tour right now.

Nicklaus was the Tiger Woods of his day in terms of length. He routinely outdrove other pros by 30 yards, and it was because of what you see here (in frames 1 and 2). Nicklaus got his hands very far from his body early in the swing, which gave him lots of time to generate clubhead speed. The trick was to get that great extension without swaying off the ball or shifting his weight outside of his feet. These photos are of Nicklaus as a senior, but he still has the great extension. Webb gets similar extension—and Woods looks this way at this point in the swing

as well—and she reaps the benefits in her long game.

The most idiosynchratic part of Nicklaus' swing was the "flying elbow." At the top of his backswing, Nicklaus' hands are so far above his head, he couldn't help but let his right elbow drift away from his body. But when the club is halfway down, the elbow is back in perfect position. Webb's elbow flies a little bit as well, but, like Nicklaus, she's in perfect position.

The elbow is tucked at her side, and her body is ready to transmit the fierce whipping action through impact. Both Nicklaus and Webb are able to drive their hands straight down from the top of the backswing with the clubhead trailing behind, then release into the ball. By the time Webb's hands have reached her belt on the downswing, the clubhead is still at less than a 90-degree angle to the ground. The clubhead moves so fast from this point to impact that *Golf Digest*'s high-speed camera can't catch it.

John Daly and Laura Davies

THE COMPARISON BETWEEN THE SWINGS OF JOHN DALY and Laura Davies is an irresistible one. Both come as close to swinging at maximum power with the driver as any professional player, and both are virtually self-taught. Daly and Davies also have swings that match their on-course personas—hit it, find it, then hit it again. Both have terrific short games, so they rely on aggressive, risk-reward tee shots to bite off big chunks of yardage. Their philosophy? A 65-yard flip wedge—even from the rough—is better than a 140-yard shot from the middle of the fairway.

At the top of the backswing, Davies' position is only slightly less freakish than Daly's. Davies has fully cocked her left knee to get as much shoulder turn as she can, and the club has gone way past parallel. Daly has incredible flexibility—he's able to turn his shoulders so that his back is actually facing to the right of the target—and he has the same dramatic knee cock as Davies. Daly is able to get the club so far behind him that it points down over his left shoulder at the ball. No other top-flight professional golfer has ever gotten this much coil. Only long-drive competition guys do this. Davies doesn't get the club quite as far past parallel, but she's still in a position unique among female professionals. It is because of this position, along with her size, that Davies can carry the ball 275 yards with the driver.

From the top, both players start unwinding their hips as fast as they can. At impact, you can see how both have turned their hips well past the ball and toward the target, ahead of the arms swinging through. Both Daly and Davies have their heads well behind the ball and are hitting against a rock-solid left side.

Even with the huge swing, Daly is in very good balance at impact, and he is never out of control. Davies only looks like she has lost control—at impact she's up on her toes because of the downward force of her swing. The position of both Daly's and Davies' head at impact is also strikingly similar. Both keep their head stable, looking down at the ball, until the arms and shoulders have passed by on the way to the follow-through. Without this kind of solid pivot point, big swings like these would fly out of control.

Frame 1

Frame 2

Frame 1

Frame 2

Sergio Garcia and Ben Hogan

WHEN SERGIO GARCIA BROKE ONTO THE SCENE AT THE 1999 PGA by taking Tiger Woods down to the 72nd hole, the golf public was enchanted with his personality, but also intrigued with his unique golf swing. It certainly looked familiar, and it should. Garcia's incredible lag and squatting position at impact are reminiscent of another small man who used physics to get the most from his swing—Ben Hogan.

Hogan generated incredible wrist cock early in the downswing, then held this angle until his hands were down near his belt buckle. The clubhead then exploded into the ball. Most players before—and since—have the club at a 90-degree angle to the left arm at this point. The only player to recreate that Hogan lag faithfully—and control it well enough to win at the highest level—has been Garcia. Garcia looks like a Hogan clone here, with the same kind of dramatic wrist cock. By the time Garcia's hands are halfway through the downswing, the clubhead is still behind his back. He generates incredible clubhead speed for a man of his size. He routinely hits 300-yard drives and carries his 6-iron 200 yards.

Hogan and Garcia also have another very similar aspect of their swings. At the top of the backswing, both men squat slightly and keep separation between their knees. Hogan said he wanted to feel like he was gripping the ground with his feet to anchor his swing. Hogan and Garcia straighten from the squat at the moment of impact. The only significant difference in the two swings here is that Hogan's stance is wider. Hogan also mastered his lag through years and years of beating balls. He fanned the club open slightly on the backswing, then came through impact with it slightly open. He was doing whatever he could to avoid hitting a hook. Garcia is still perfecting his action. He has been spectacular one week, then awful the next. Ironically, the man whose swing is seen as the model for Garcia's was the opposite kind of player—relentlessly consistent.

David Duval and Grace Park

DAVID DUVAL AND GRACE PARK ARE BOTH PART OF THE newest generation of professional golfers—ones that grew up with the most advanced equipment and practice and training techiques. Both have long, athletic swings that are less-than-conventional, but still very sound. Even though they both have thoroughly modern swings, they both were taught in a way that is very familiar to one of the great players in the game's history. Jack Grout taught Jack Nicklaus to hit the ball hard, then worry about accuracy. David Duval's father, Senior Tour player Bob Duval, gave his son the same lesson. Grace Park was doing the same thing—getting the most from her small frame with an athletic move through the ball and great leverage.

The first frames shown here, halfway through the downswing, show why Duval and Park are both very long off the tee. Duval has his hips cleared past the ball and open to the target already, and the club is trailing behind. Park has less clearing of her hips, but her clubhead lags even further behind. Both players play with a very strong grip. You can see the bend in both players' left wrists, cupping outward away from the handle. At address, this hand was on top of the grip, and now it leads through impact to keep the clubhead square.

After impact, you can see where the swings start to diverge. Park needs to add some zip at the bottom of her swing to get the distance she gets out of such a small frame. She snaps her wrists through impact in this sequence, which gives her more clubhead speed, but also less control. Duval sets up with a very strong grip, fires his hips through impact and just holds on. He's doing nothing with his hands. His body rotation provides all of the clubhead speed. In college, Duval was as long as Tiger Woods is now. He's dialed it back a little bit since he joined the PGA Tour, but Duval is still one of the ten longest players on the tour. Park led the field at the 2000 Women's US Open in driving, averaging more than 300 yards per poke. Her coach, Mike LaBauve, said Park has another ten or 15 yards in reserve that she doesn't usually tap in tournament situations. "She's as long as she needs to be on any hole," he said.

Frame 1

Frame 2

Frame 1

Frame 2

Greg Norman and Davis Love III

FROM THE START OF THE 1980s, TWO MEN HAVE BEEN consistently hailed as having the best combination of length and accuracy off the tee of anyone in the professional game: Greg Norman and Davis Love III.

Whatever his other failings, Norman has always been exceptionally good with his driver. Johnny Miller tells a story of being paired once with Norman during the Aussie's formative years on the Australian Tour. Miller was one of the best—and most accurate—players on the American Tour at the time. On holes where Miller used a long iron for accuracy, Norman thought nothing of hitting a driver, and he consistently clubbed shots 300 yards into ten-yard-wide slots of fairway. Love made a similar impact when he joined the PGA Tour in the mid-1980s. Long and lanky, Love smoothed 300-yard tee shots out there with his persimmon driver, and seemingly without effort.

For both men, the power comes from an impressive coiling of the upper body in relation to the hips. Both have their backs nearly facing the target at the top of the backswing, but their hips have barely turned and their heads have remained perfectly steady. The steady platform helps them to deliver the club through impact so precisely. Both Norman and Love III hit majestic, high fades off the tee that seemingly carry forever.

At impact, both men are in very similar positions. Norman's arms are fully extended, and his left leg is firmly braced. Love has tilted his right shoulder below his left, putting his head behind the ball. You can tell that the hands haven't done too much in the swing because Love's (and Norman's) left forearm nearly covers his right arm. Too much action with the right hand would cause the right forearm to show over the top of the left arm. Power puts good players in position to attack vulnerable flags, but only if the player has enough accuracy to leave the powerful drive in a fairly good position. Both Norman and Love have historically been among the PGA Tour's leaders in birdies and eagles because they have been able to take such advantage of their long, accurate drives.

Bobby Jones and Payne Stewart

BOBBY JONES' FLOWING SWING WAS MORE A MATTER of necessity than a real desire to be a stylist. Jones was trying to keep the whippy hickory shafts of his era from over-torqueing, so he tried to guide the club through impact instead of swing it through. And while technology has helped players with faster tempos—like Tom Watson, Nick Price and Jose Maria Olazabal—succeed, the modern game still has had its share of free-flowing swingers of the golf club. Johnny Miller and Tom Weiskopf succeeded Bobby Jones, and Payne Stewart, before his tragic death in 2000, took over from where Weiskopf left off.

In his first move away from the ball, Jones almost dragged the club along the ground in his effort to keep his arms, wrists and the shaft in "one piece," a solid unit. He didn't cock his wrists until his hands had past upward past his waist. Stewart didn't keep the club quite as low as Jones, but he did have a "late set," where he kept his arms, wrists and shaft as a unified unit well into the backswing. This move translated visually into a sweep of the club away from the ball. Neither man snatched the club back away from the ball abruptly or made any violent change of direction at any point in the swing.

Through impact, both men swept the club gracefully—and powerfully—into the finish. Neither man had a "hit" move at impact, like Ben Hogan or Jesper Parnevik. It's almost as if the ball got in the way of the club. In reality, the definition of a "classic" swing like that of Jones, Weiskopf or Stewart is more about the tempo than anything else. Something that looks so graceful will always be considered the best of its kind, no matter the era. The fortunate by-product of that kind of swing is that it doesn't usually require much maintenance. Both Jones and Stewart weren't notorious range rats. They hit balls only long enough to warm up and sharpen the natural "feel" and internal timing that are critical to maintaining that syrupy tempo. Once they got into the rhythm, they were ready to play. Jones often didn't play any golf over the winter, and needed only a few weeks of physical training and practice rounds to be in top championship form in the spring

Frame 1

Frame 2

Frame 1

Frame 2

Tom Watson and Nick Price

IN THEIR RESPECTIVE CAREER PEAKS, TOM WATSON AND Nick Price had many things in common. In the late 1970s, Watson used his fast-tempo swing and crisp ball-striking to great effect, while he aggressively rammed in birdie putts. Price had his own run in the early 1990s, winning back-to-back PGAs and a British Open with his fast-tempo, pure-strike swing. He was also an aggressive putter. While both men had tempos that were much faster than the average tour player's, they both were considered the preeminent ball-strikers of their times. Why? Because their technique was very good and their tempo was consistent throughout the swing—equally fast through the backswing and through the downswing.

In addition to having similar tempos, Watson and Price have similar swings. Price is slightly more upright at the top of the backswing and Watson turns a little more fully and releases his right elbow from his side slightly, but both men make a dramatic weight shift to the right leg. Watson's right leg is almost straight. But both men have the club in perfect position, pointing parallel to the target line.

Past impact, both men have kept their heads very steady and have allowed the hips and shoulders to unwind under and through. In both photgraphs, you can see how well they have braced the left leg to allow the right side to pivot around. Firm resistance in both the backswing and downswing means that neither man shifts his weight outside his feet—a major consistency killer common in the swings of many average amateurs. By pivoting instead of sliding, Watson and Price transmit all of their swing speed into the ball and waste nothing.

Acknowledgements

I couldn't have finished this book without the help of two people: my patient wife,
Fernanda, and Ed Weathers, my editor at *Golf Digest*. Fernanda kept me pointed in the
right direction, and Ed's keen eye and soft editing touch made me a better writer.
I'd also like to thank all of the other *Golf Digest* editors, players and instructors
who created the original magazine stories on which this book is based.
Their good work made my job easy.

Matt Rudy, 2001